Battling Demon Rum

BATTLING
DEMON RUM

The Struggle for a
Dry America, 1800–1933

Thomas R. Pegram

The American Ways Series

IVAN R. DEE   *Chicago*

Library of Congress Cataloging-in-Publication Data:
Pegram, Thomas R., 1955–
    Battling demon rum : the struggle for a dry America, 1800–1933 / Thomas R. Pegram.
       p. cm. —— (The American ways series)
    Includes bibliographical references and index.
    ISBN 1-56663-208-0 (cloth : alk. paper). — ISBN 1-56663-209-9 (pbk. : alk. paper)
    1. Temperance—United States—History. 2. Alcoholism—United States—Prevention—History. 3. Prohibition—United States—History. 4. Liquor laws—United States—History. I. Title.
    II. Series.
HV5292.P44   1998
363.4'1'0973—dc21   98-15875

For Patty, Tavish, and Rafe

Contents

Preface

IN 1758 a prominent Virginia politician spent thirty-seven pounds, seven shillings to win a seat in the House of Burgesses. Nearly all of it went for "brandy, rum, cyder, strong beer, and wine" distributed to freeholders on the day of the election. The politician was George Washington, and he understood that even in the deferential political system of colonial Virginia, voters required gestures of liberality, even of service, from the gentlemen who governed over them. By "treating" voters with strong drink, candidates reinforced the public nature and community significance of elections, acknowledged the value of citizenship, and, not so subtly, reminded freeholders of their political obligations to community leaders. Alcohol was a *presence* in American politics, part of its mechanism, long before it became an *issue* to be resolved.

In 1912 a humbler observer in Peru, Illinois, testified to the continuing importance of alcohol in modern mass-democratic politics. "You know as well as I do," confided small-time political operative John Owiecki to a prospective governor, "it takes the price of [a] little beer to talk politikes." To some of the miners, farmers, and mechanics who received beer and cigars from political canvassers such as Owiecki, the treating ritual reflected the sensibilities of democracy. It emphasized sociability, denied class distinctions, and embodied the widespread belief that the principal function of government, through the agency of political parties, was to distribute goods, services, and privileges to American citizens. In short, the public exchange of alcoholic beverages during elections celebrated the political culture of a free people.

To many other Americans, however, the treating custom represented the very negation of democracy. They saw it as a bold maneuver by selfish politicians to manipulate the vote of any man cynical, weak, dissolute, or apathetic enough to be corrupted by a false show of fraternity and a cheap shot of whiskey or a draft of beer. Critics of treating measured the disabling impact of alcohol on politics by the ragged November marches of hoboes, drifters, and beaten-down men from Chicago alderman Michael "Hinky Dink" Kenna's Workingmen's Exchange and a thousand similar establishments to the nation's polling places. The place of alcohol in American democracy had become an urgent and bitterly contentious public issue.

In politics as in private life, depending upon the context of its use, alcohol has helped build communities or subvert them. As "the good creature of God" celebrated by Puritan minister Increase Mather, strong drink was a constant and valued symbol of shared human ties. Americans have used alcohol to salute personal achievements, seal agreements, mark the solemnity of religious rites, celebrate the events that bound together families and communities, and, sometimes, to overcome the awkward silences between strangers. The culture of public drinking in taverns and clubs has also produced political activism, from the public houses of revolutionary America to the Stonewall Inn, the 1969 birthplace of the modern gay rights movement. In the late eighteenth century American taverns were symbols of resistance to the British imperial system. Colonists brawled with British soldiers around the liberty poles that stood in front of many public houses. Inside the taverns, the air of rough male egalitarianism also prompted resistance to traditional patterns of deference in ways that suggested the struggle for independence could also be revolutionary. The male-centered political culture of Revolutionary Era taverns prefigured nineteenth-century American democracy, which celebrated universal white manhood suffrage as its central achievement. Serving as a polling place and the site of political meetings, guarded by the Jacksonian slogan of personal liberty, the American saloon became a powerful symbol of freedom and egalitarianism to many Americans and a fitting icon of American democracy.

But in the estimation of many men and women, alcohol had a destructive impact on American society. Squandered wages, neglected or abused families, moral degeneration, crime, poverty, and disease were some of the costs of personal intemperance. In the public sphere, a political culture that often defined freedom and equality by the conviviality of the barroom was, in the eyes of its detractors, too willing to defend liberty at the expense of progress, to prize democratic participation as long as it excluded women and blacks, and to elevate individualism above the common good. Seen from this perspective, drinking created personal and political deviancy.

My purpose here is to examine the relationship between American political institutions and temperance reform, that broad effort to reduce or eliminate altogether the manufacture, sale, and use of beverage alcohol. Temperance reform was a powerful and revealing American social movement that lasted from roughly 1800 until the repeal of the 18th Amendment in 1933 ended national prohibition. Many nineteenth-century Americans believed passionately that drinking ruined lives and disrupted society. Over time, many more came to believe that the alcohol industry—the brewers and distillers that manufactured strong drink and the saloons in which it was sold—directly and intentionally threatened the family, the social order, and democracy itself.

Some combated the menace of alcohol in voluntary, essentially private ways known as moral suasion. Moral suasionists set personal examples of sobriety for family and friends, educated children to exercise self-control and abhor drunkenness, or encouraged drinkers to break free of their addiction. But the best-organized and most persistent temperance reformers advocated public remedies; they arranged street demonstrations, formed political parties, and built sophisticated pressure groups intent on using the power of government to regulate and ultimately prohibit access to alcohol. Prohibitionist influence crested twice during the period: first, in a short-lived proliferation of prohibition statutes in the North and Midwest modeled on Maine's pioneering 1851 law and, second, in a burst of prohibition triumphs between 1907 and World War I which resulted in the 1919 adoption of a prohibition amendment to the United States Constitution.

Real rather than imagined problems prompted the activism of temperance reformers. Alcohol consumption increased alarmingly in the early years of the nineteenth century, and family violence and public disorder became more noticeable in its wake. Many saloons were indeed squalid places where men defied the conventions of Victorian sentimentality and where, near the end of the century, saloonkeeper-politicians held sway. The liquor industry acted with the arrogance typical of corporations in the age of capital. These concerns pointed to more basic issues of power, culture, and authority in American public life. In a densely multi-ethnic society in which radically different attitudes toward alcohol contended, temperance debates reflected the struggle over whose cultural standards should be sanctioned in the public life of the nation. In a political order dominated by men and mainstream political parties, temperance reform became a means by which women and political outsiders acted to defend their interests and assert their influence. Finally, in a governmental system that aimed to balance the countervailing values of liberty and order, support for tougher liquor regulation pushed many Americans to accept an expansion of government authority over individual (and corporate) behavior. Temperance reform thus played a role in the growth of the modern American state. The repeal of prohibition, in turn, has been a reminder of the limitations and dangers of government intervention in general and moral regulation in particular. For more than sixty years, Americans have lived with that odd, ambiguous legacy of hesitant activism.

The interplay between temperance reformers, political parties, and government identifies strains and alterations in the American political system during a turbulent period of national growth and upheaval. The methods by which Americans organized to further temperance, and the measures they advocated to bring it about, reflected new approaches to political action and shifting expectations of government. Although the *regulation* of alcohol was a standard governmental responsibility in the United States, American political parties and public officials shied away from more coercive measures such as prohibition. Moreover, party leaders feared that temperance questions cut across customary lines of partisan division and created instability. The surges of prohibitionist sentiment in the 1850s and at the turn of the century came at moments of particular crisis for American political parties. During each decade, ordinary citizens complained that parties avoided issues that mattered and were without principles. Major political realignments and demands for activist government quickly followed. High points in temperance activism, it seems, also indicate key moments of change in American politics.

On the other hand, the inability to *enforce* prohibition effectively during the 1850s and the 1920s suggests the enormous difference between creating public policy and actually governing. Without the stability furnished by deeply rooted political parties, even the best-organized popular reform movements are overmatched. The temperance movement often overextended itself during periods of political emergency—first, upon the breakup of political parties during the 1850s and, later, during the feverish political atmosphere surrounding American entry into World War I. In both cases prohibition laws passed quickly without the usual restraining influence of political parties. But in the face of strong opposition, such laws could not be drawn up or enforced without the prestige and resources of political parties. The parties had not invested heavily in prohibition and so had little stake in its failure. In our current political age of active pressure groups, lobbyists, and single-interest associations, it is wise to remember that political parties, now supposedly in decline, are still necessary for government to function.

My friend and colleague J. Matthew Gallman suggested that I write this book. For that, and for the example of his own excellent contribution to the American Ways series, I thank him. John Braeman and Ivan Dee offered astute editorial judgment and demonstrated great patience as this study took shape. Dean David Roswell of Loyola College provided crucial support which allowed me to continue writing. The Inter-Library Loan office at the Loyola–Notre Dame Library efficiently obtained books for me. Although I did some original research for this book, a synthetic work of this type depends utterly on the labors of other scholars. I would like to salute them, especially those on whom I have most heavily relied: Jack Blocker, Ian Tyrrell, W. J. Rorabaugh, J. C. Burnham,

Austin Kerr, James Timberlake, Norman Clark, Richard
Hamm, and David Kyvig. My colleagues in the history department at Loyola College kindly read and discussed one of
the chapters. Beyond that, their spirit of scholarly good fellowship help make work fun. Elaine Parsons generously took
time from her dissertation to read and comment on a chapter.
No one read more of this book nor did more to make it clear
and focused than Patricia Ingram. Raymond and Dorothy Pegram and Pearl Ingram politely impressed upon me the advantages of finishing this project. Tavish and Rafferty Pegram
delayed the completion of the book but made the process infi-
nitely sweeter.

T. R. P.

Baltimore, Maryland
May 1998

Battling Demon Rum

1

Drinking and Temperance in the Age of Reform

ALCOHOL became an American problem between 1790 and 1830, during the expansive years of the early republic. Drinking, long accepted as an essential component of daily life and social interaction, in that period began to be seen as a cause of disorder and a barrier to progress. Organized efforts to promote temperance appeared in the 1820s as part of the extraordinary outburst of reform activism that transformed the United States in the first half of the nineteenth century. Inspired by religious enthusiasm, democratic hopes, and moral concerns, temperance reformers joined sabbatarians, abolitionists, women's rights advocates, pacifists, and crusaders for reform in health, education, and the treatment of disease, crime, and poverty in ambitious efforts to improve and even perfect American society. Imbued with the ideals of democratic individualism and expectations for the establishment of a Christian republic, most early temperance reformers emphasized self-control for the temperate and self-improvement for the troubled drinker. But the persistence of social disorder tied to drink, and anxieties associated with increased immigration and economic downturns, influenced temperance organizations in the 1830s and 1840s to demand that the power of law and the authority of the state be used to force temperance onto those who refused to adopt it voluntarily. This blending of optimism, anxiety, and the willingness to use coercion in the service of reform thereafter marked the relationship between temperance reform and American politics.

The expansion of American democracy, ripe with the promise of liberty yet potentially disruptive of individual lives and the established social order, set the context for temperance reform. In the wake of the Revolution, Americans questioned and in some cases cast off traditional forms of authority. In politics, religion, and social organization, they struggled to create institutions fit for a free people. Population tripled, from 3,929,000 in 1790 to 12,901,000 in 1830. Cities grew larger, more numerous, and more dangerous. Settlers surged into the Midwest and onto the Southern frontier, bringing new states into the Union and upsetting the political dominance of the Atlantic seaboard. As the nation's commercial infrastructure matured with the development of roads, steamboats, and canals, the market revolution brought most Americans into the cash economy. Relations between employers and workers shifted. Americans in small towns and in the countryside found that the prosperity of their families depended on the location of transportation routes, the tastes and purchasing power of city dwellers, and the fluctuations of foreign markets. It was an age of buoyancy and opportunity, of expanded hopes, but many Americans also felt unsettled and anxious during this period of swift change.

The astute French observer of American life, Alexis de Tocqueville, noted in the 1830s the "strange unrest of so many happy men." "In the United States," he wrote, "a man builds a house in which to spend his old age, and he sells it before the roof is on; he plants a garden and lets it just as the trees are coming into bearing; he brings a field into tillage and leaves other men to gather the crops; he embraces a profession and gives it up; he settles in a place, which he soon afterwards leaves to carry his changeable longings elsewhere." Americans embraced liberty with enthusiasm but seemed skittish and impulsive in its exercise.

As Americans explored the physical dimensions of liberty in the early republic, they also struggled with the consequences of self-government. On the one hand—in a position first outlined by Alexander Hamilton and later expanded upon by Whigs such as Henry Clay—some Americans stressed the ability of government, if guided by wise laws and intelligent leaders, to promote national growth, encourage moral improvement, and develop virtuous and productive citizens capable of governing the republic. This viewpoint, at least implicitly, recognized a hierarchy of talent and temperament in public as well as in private life, and encouraged the rational restraint of antisocial impulses. Others put their faith in limited government, expanded democracy, and individual freedom to pursue one's self-interest. The "contagion of liberty" that followed the establishment of American independence spilled into the nineteenth century as vigilant republicans, invoking the principles of Thomas Jefferson and then the leadership of Andrew Jackson, criticized symbols of elitism and privilege and worked to bring them under democratic control. State-supported churches were disestablished and local judges made subject to popular election; formal requirements governing entry into the professions were relaxed, and deference to the "natural leadership" of great men was challenged. By the 1820s the traditional state-imposed property qualifications that restricted the electorate at the end of the eighteenth century had given way to universal suffrage for

adult white men. Between 1820 and 1830 the number of qual-
ified voters in the United States doubled. Deferential representative politics had been replaced by mass democracy.

The passage from deferential to mass-democratic politics
was not initially smooth. Between 1790 and 1815, sharp differ-
ences over fundamental principles lent a bitter, combative tone
to politics. One of the first forceful acts of the national government under the Constitution, Hamilton's attempt to tax the
production of whiskey, prompted armed resistance on the part
of western Pennsylvania farmers in 1794 and necessitated the
use of military force to crush the rebellion. John Adams and
Thomas Jefferson, who together wrote the Declaration of Independence in 1776, denounced each other as enemies of the
nation as they fought for the presidency in 1800. Jefferson's
supporters reviled Adams as a dictator and toady of the
British monarch while Federalists reproached Jefferson as
"Mad Tom"—an atheist, a demagogue, and an apologist for
the wildest excesses of the French Revolution. Partisan rancor
eased after 1800, but disputes stemming from foreign policy
threatened national unity until the conclusion of the War of
1812. The New England states resisted Jefferson's 1807 embargo on trade with the European powers, opposed war with
Great Britain in 1812, and remained coolly resistant to patriotic enthusiasm during the ensuing conflict. Yet American
democracy weathered its early crisis, and when Jefferson and
Adams, by then reconciled after years of ill feeling, both died
on July 4, 1826, a nation attuned to omens interpreted the
event as a sign of God's approbation of American democracy
and special intentions for the republic.

But the shining potential of American democracy was
threatened in the eyes of many by the empire of King Alcohol.
Aided by the growth of the market economy and its attendant
dislocations, Americans between 1800 and 1830 drank more

alcohol, on an individual basis, than at any other time in the history of the nation. During that span Americans above the age of fourteen on average consumed each year between 6.6 and 7.1 gallons of pure alcohol (current American consumption is about 2.8 gallons annually). Because of the decline in deference and the new democratic hostility to restraints on liberty, they also drank without customary controls and in different ways than they had before. In the eyes of some observers, nineteenth-century America had become a "nation of drunkards."

The identification of alcohol as a social problem in the early nineteenth century marked an important change in American attitudes toward strong drink. Alcoholic beverages had been present as an essential component of life from the establishment of the first colonial settlements in North America. When the Puritan settlers of the Massachusetts Bay Colony dropped anchor in 1630, 12 gallons of distilled spirits, 10,000 gallons of beer, and 120 hogsheads of brewing malt arrived with them. By the eighteenth century Americans not only brewed beer—ranging from a hearty barley brew containing 6 percent alcohol to the more common 1 percent "small beer"— for home consumption but made widespread use of local fruits and grains to produce hard cider (7 percent alcohol) and more powerful distilled liquor such as applejack, peach brandy, and corn and rye whiskey (40 percent alcohol or higher). The New England trade with the West Indies provided molasses which spurred rum production in coastal towns. Although community scorn and the power of law was brought to bear on drunkards, everyone was expected to consume alcoholic beverages as dietary staples, and overindulgence was tolerated at weddings, funerals, militia musters, and on holidays. Women drank in the home; men drank more frequently and more copiously at home, in the fields or the

shop, and at taverns and during public events such as elections; solicitous parents shared beer with children at meals and
encouraged boys to develop a taste for distilled spirits.

Between 1800 and 1830 the use of alcohol was so basic a
component of daily life that strong drink could be found in
every conceivable situation. In the 1790s President John
Adams enjoyed a tankard of hard cider with his breakfast
every morning. Each family in a group traveling by wagon to
Indianapolis in 1823 drained a half-gallon of whiskey daily as
they bounced along the trail. Horace Greeley, the influential
American editor, recalled of his Vermont boyhood around
1820 that "there was no merry-making, there was no entertainment of relatives or friends, there was scarcely a casual
gathering of two or three neighbors for an evening's social
chat, without strong drink." Eastern farmhands customarily
received a half-pint to a pint of rum daily as they worked the
fields; artisans put down their tools for drams twice daily; soldiers and sailors were issued daily rations of rum or whiskey.
Even clergymen drank, sometimes to excess. One temperance-
minded minister complained that fellow churchmen attending an ordination made such liberal use of alcoholic provisions
that the sideboard "looked and smelled like the bar of a very
active grog-shop."

Many early temperance advocates denounced only distilled
liquor (whiskey, rum, gin, and other spirits that contained between 40 and 50 percent alcohol) and continued to drink fermented alcohol (beer, hard cider, and wine, all with a natural
alcoholic content of 12 percent or less). Huntington Lyman, a
prominent evangelist, remembered as a boy fetching a bar-
rowful of beer for a meeting at which Congregationalist ministers resolved to "preach against the extravagant use of rum."
The Massachusetts Society for the Suppression of Intemper-

ance, one of the first prominent temperance organizations, served wine at its gatherings.

Americans drank because they believed that, when taken in moderate doses, alcohol was not only safe but actually beneficial to their health. In the early nineteenth century most Americans frequently worked outdoors. The warm feeling produced by a cup of rum or whiskey convinced laborers and travelers that liquor offered necessary protection from the elements. It was also commonly believed that alcohol possessed rejuvenative powers that helped workers carry out heavy or toilsome labor. Americans preferred to drink spirits because distilled liquor was safer, more plentiful, and cheaper than alternative beverages. Water was held in low regard as a beverage in the early nineteenth century. Even when clean it was thought to have no nutritional or digestive value. Most water available for drinking, however, was muddy, brackish, metallic-tasting, or had to be obtained by means of wells, long hauls, or frequent rain. The supply of milk was inconsistent and extremely perishable. Beer did not keep well, and wine was uncommon. Coffee and tea were expensive, whereas whiskey was pure, pleasurable, and in the 1820s cost twenty-five cents per gallon.

The cheap price of whiskey was a consequence of American expansion and a major reason for the increase in alcohol consumption between 1800 and 1830. Americans spilling over the Appalachian Mountains into the Ohio country and the southern interior found that their corn and rye was cheaper to ship to market in the form of whiskey than as grain. Politics also aided the rise of whiskey. High tariffs and strained trade relations with Great Britain cut off supplies of West Indian molasses, crippling rum production, and in 1802 the whiskey excise tax was repealed. By 1820 American drinkers were enjoying a whiskey glut; whiskey and cider stood supreme as the national beverages.

After 1800 drinking also took place in a different behavioral context. Liquor had traditionally been drunk in the United States in moderate doses, or drams, throughout the day in the company of family members or fellow workers, punctuated by excessive drinking at communal celebrations several times each year. According to the historian W. J. Rorabaugh, the chief authority on American drinking patterns in the nineteenth century, the 1820s witnessed a shift to more frequent binge drinking, both solitary and with companions. Americans, especially white men, drank hard liquor to the point of drunkenness with greater frequency. Rorabaugh attributed this development to the impact of rapid economic and social change and the culture of mass democracy.

The shifting relationship between employers and artisans provides an illustration. Before the effects of the industrial revolution began to be felt in the early nineteenth century, journeymen who worked in small shops could hope someday to become masters owning their own shops. The rise of the factory system formalized the relationships between employer and employee and diminished the probability of economic advancement. Rorabaugh found that frustrated workers demanded expanded drinking privileges on the job and battled with employers over shop drinking policies. Alcohol, which had been a symbol of steady habits and a brotherhood of craftsmanship, now became a tool of resistance, a companion in despair, and a belligerent affirmation of liberty. The rowdy drinking practices of canal workers shared this spirit of protest and affirmation. Hard-driven and relatively powerless in the workplace, canal workers expressed their refusal to be dominated by asserting control over their leisure time. Canal-men's legendary binges not only provided a boisterous refuge from their rough employment but defiantly proclaimed that they alone would set the standards of their personal conduct.

After 1800 the connections between a male culture of drinking and the expression of democratic citizenship also grew more prominent. Although all Americans drank, men by far were the heaviest imbibers. Rorabaugh estimated that in the late 1820s half the adult males in the population consumed two-thirds of the distilled spirits. With increasing frequency, men did a portion of their drinking in taverns or at work, out of the company of wives and children. Regular public access to alcohol became one of the prerogatives of citizenship. The relaxation of eighteenth-century tavern regulations meant that legal and customary restraints on the consumption of alcohol bore down most visibly on noncitizens: slaves, children, and women. Drinking by slaves was controlled by statute law and the will of slaveowners, who doled out spirits during harvests and for Christmas sprees. Women and children were barred by custom from taverns and did most of their drinking in the home. The rise of domesticity in the nineteenth century solidified expectations of virtue and restraint for female behavior and closed women off from active participation in the public world of drink and fraternity.

Changes in the regulation of public drinking reflected the decline of deference and the enthusiasm for liberty that marked the onset of mass democracy. Colonial law had regulated taverns to various degrees. Distinctions were made between public houses, which provided accommodations to travelers and were allowed to serve strong drink, and retail liquor shops, which sold jugs and bottles to be consumed elsewhere. In some locales, tavernkeepers were barred from selling to confirmed drunkards. "Tippling" laws specified how long townspeople could drink in taverns; a Connecticut

statute from the early nineteenth century forced drinkers to
move on after an hour. But Americans increasingly shrugged
off such restraints on individual behavior. Westward expansion and the proliferation of taverns on the frontier made regulation modeled on colonial communities unsuitable. Existing
laws fell into disuse as free men dismantled the structure of
eighteenth-century authority. Even informal controls on
drinking became outmoded in the changing American social
landscape. When workers boarded in the house of their employer, as was common before the sharp changes of the 1820s,
their behavior came under watchful eyes. The new industrial
relations of the nineteenth century moved workers out of the
sight and the moral authority of employers. Both by intent
and by happenstance, Americans were on their own when it
came to drinking.

The culture of drinking that permeated American society between 1800 and 1830 reflected both anxiety and optimism.
Rapid social change and the instability of fortunes drove many
Americans to the bottle with greater frequency. At other times
Americans drank to assert their independence, their egalitar-
ian ideals, and their status as citizens in a democracy. The
same factors influenced the temperance movement, which
worked to curb the outburst of drinking that after 1800 became so visible. Fear of disorder and anxiety over the fate of
the family, the moral order, and the nation itself prompted
temperance activism. The frequency of street and tavern riots
in New York City, for instance, escalated steadily after 1800,
then between 1825 and 1829 surged to a stunning figure of
sixty-three disturbances. Anarchy seemed to prevail in neighborhoods such as the city's notorious Five Points slum, where
the streets bristled with groceries and taverns packed with
"drinking, swearing, and fighting" patrons.

Public violence and the routine display in cities of the effects of alcoholic dissipation drove some worried Americans toward temperance as a defensive measure. But for many others, temperance reform was a supremely confident, hopeful movement, reflecting the buoyant faith that Americans, by their own actions, could perfect their society. During the great push for improvement in the first half of the nineteenth century, temperance, in the assessment of the historian Steven Mintz, was "the unifying reform, drawing support from countless middle-class Protestants, from skilled artisans, clerks, shopkeepers, laborers, free blacks, and Mormons, as well as from many conservative clergy and southerners who were otherwise hostile to reform." It also became a major vehicle for women's activism. In that sense, temperance was also an expression of democracy.

The first stirrings of anti-liquor sentiment that can be connected to the emergence of the temperance movement in the 1820s took place in the 1780s. Quakers and Methodists, denominations that had long counseled caution in the use of distilled liquor, sharply intensified their hostility to spirits during that decade of American independence, demanding that church members stop participating in the liquor trade and condemning the personal consumption of ardent spirits. In 1784 Dr. Benjamin Rush, signer of the Declaration of Independence and former surgeon general of the Continental Army, published his influential temperance tract, *An Inquiry into the Effects of Spirituous Liquors upon the Human Body, and Their Influence upon the Happiness of Society*, which would circulate for years in pamphlet form as a forceful expression of new, more critical attitudes toward the use of alcohol. Key features that would distinguish early-nineteenth-century temperance reform were already present in the views of Rush and the church bodies. They both considered distilled liquors to be dangerous but sanctioned the use of fermented drinks such as beer, wine, and cider. They advised personal abstinence from distilled liquors but not legal prohibition. Finally, they looked beyond the ruined lives of individual drunkards to insist that intemperance threatened the social order itself. Their religious, moral, and medical arguments were aimed primarily at changing the behavior of moderate drinkers so as to undermine the American culture of drinking.

Rush in particular linked the effects of strong drink on the human body to its larger impact on the fortunes of the newly independent republic. Dedicated to the success of the new nation, he suggested education policies, dietary principles, and behavioral norms suitable for the cultivation of virtuous citizens. His commitment to temperance fit the same purpose. In the *Inquiry*, Rush broke with mainstream medical opinion by denying the health-giving properties of alcohol. To the contrary, he claimed that the alcohol in distilled liquor (Rush shared the common view that fermented drinks were free of the damaging effects of alcohol) upset the body's internal balance and over time produced physical disease and behavioral vices such as idleness, fighting, swearing, and criminality. The chronic use of spirits broke down the body and corroded the virtues necessary to sustain self-government. Rush devised a "Moral and Physical Thermometer" to illustrate the progressive deterioration of health and morals caused by intemperance and included it in later editions of the *Inquiry*. In the 1790 version, chronic intemperance led not only to melancholy, madness, and jail time but to anarchy and hatred of just government. If the American culture of drinking were to grow unchecked, Rush feared the onset of a government "chosen by intemperate and corrupted voters." Without a virtuous citizenry, "the republic would soon be in danger." Thus to Rush, beer and cider were "invaluable FEDERAL liquors" which promoted cheerfulness and political stability as against the "Antifederal" influence of ardent spirits, "companions of all those vices that are calculated to dishonor and enslave our country."

Elite concern over the moral and political order prompted the organization of the earliest nineteenth-century temperance societies. The first association founded exclusively to promote temperance, the Massachusetts Society for the Suppression of Intemperance (MSSI), took shape in 1813 amid economic and political turbulence. Before 1800 the Bay State was notable for its commercial prosperity, the influence exercised by its Congregationalist clergy (including orthodox Calvinists and rationalist Unitarians who, after 1805, would break away to establish their own denomination), and the political authority of its Federalist party. Jefferson's embargo and the War of 1812 spread economic hardship through coastal communities, hampering trade, driving down population, and increasing the strain on the poorhouses. The decline of deference brought sharp challenges in religion from dissenting sects, primarily Baptists and Methodists, and in politics from Jeffersonian Republicans who drew upon the support of religious dissenters and modest property holders to win several elections after 1807.

The MSSI represented an attempt by an embattled elite to protect public virtue from the corruption of popular intemperance. Its exclusive organization consisted of a parent society in Boston and some forty auxiliary bodies in neighboring towns; members were elected and paid annual dues of two dollars. They were mostly prosperous men, members of the Congregational or Unitarian churches, and overwhelmingly Federalist in their political convictions. Although the MSSI stressed the desirability for temperance among its members, its chief concern was in curbing lower-class drinking and the social disorder that stemmed from "the misrule of sordid appetite." To that end the MSSI encouraged employers to stop furnishing spirits to their workers and pressed local and state authorities to enforce tavern regulations, crack down on illegal dramshops that sold liquor by the drink, and carefully review license holders.

In the end, however, the MSSI proved itself out of step with the temperance innovations of the nineteenth century. Rather than zealously seeking out converts and spreading its message through pamphlets, handbills, and other printed materials, the MSSI restricted its membership and issued few publications. Although it stressed the need for law enforcement, it did not act forcefully to bring about policy changes. Instead the MSSI relied on the prestige of its membership to influence public affairs and private behavior. It sought to instill deference rather than self-control. In short, the MSSI fought the democratic spirit of the age instead of reflecting it. By 1818 the association was in serious decline; by 1823 it had practically disappeared. In that year MSSI leaders acknowledged defeat.

Ten years after the failure of the MSSI, one million Americans enrolled in more than six thousand voluntary associations had pledged themselves to abstain totally from the use of spirits. A revolution in temperance sentiment had occurred. The emergence of temperance reform as a mass movement in the 1820s exuded optimism as much as it reflected anxiety over the fate of individuals and the nation. Temperance reformers celebrated free will to the same extent that they required adherence to social duty. Most of all, temperance reform in the 1820s demanded immediate and life-altering action.

The contradictory impact of the market revolution advanced these developments. On the one hand, changing economic circumstances prompted men to drink more, either to assert their independence or to oppose their deteriorating status in the new order. But the market revolution also put a premium on sobriety, order, and rationality and offered to reward dedicated effort. However substantial their fear of disorder or their wish to control the behavior of others, most temperance advocates confidently embraced the ideology of progress and the promise of opportunity in an expansive society. Merchants and manufacturers stopped drinking in order to take up the discipline of the market revolution, and they encouraged their workers to internalize the same traits of sober self-control. A New York farmer who stopped providing whiskey to his hands proudly reported that they "labored like sober, rational men, and not like intoxicated mutineers." In the South, temperance sentiment was strongest among middle-class town dwellers and skilled workers in Virginia, Georgia, and North Carolina. It languished in the hinterland, where the market revolution had not penetrated. Visions of progress for families as well as fears of violence and poverty at the hands of drunken husbands inspired many women to undertake temperance activism. To use the terminology of the historian Ian Tyrrell, temperance attracted improvers—men and women who acted on their faith in the future.

The upsurge in the popularity of temperance reform was deeply influenced by the spirit, message, and methods of the Second Great Awakening, a series of religious revivals that swept through the United States between 1795 and 1837. Growing out of specific local circumstances, doctrinal disputes within the established churches, and the overall rootlessness of the age, the revivals roared through regions where the dislocations accompanying social change were most pronounced: first the frontier, then western New York along the path of the Erie Canal, and finally New England. The new evangelical thrust of the Awakening—emphasizing the need for personal, emotional contact with God—spurned the passive Christian-

ity of orthodox Calvinism, with its learned theological debates
and distant impersonal Deity. The revivalists offered thousands of Americans the chance to seize control of their lives by
embracing salvation through dramatic personal acts of conversion. The age of democratic individualism found its religious parallel in the revivals as sinners chose to be saved.

Charles Grandison Finney, the Presbyterian evangelist
whose fiery revivals from 1823 to 1831 reduced western New
York to a "burned-over district," was the chief exponent of an
active Christianity that soon invigorated secular reform. "Religion is something to do," he stressed, "not something to wait
for." Once converted, Christians should work to improve their
world, both out of altruism and to hasten Christ's Second
Coming. Most nineteenth-century American evangelicals
were postmillennialists, that is, they believed that Christ
would return to earth *after* the churches had stamped out immorality and defeated evil. This doctrine emphasized the per-
fectibility of humankind but also underlined the impossibility
of tolerating wickedness. To zealous Christians, secular reform became a critical accompaniment of religious expression.
As Finney put it, "their spirit is necessarily that of the reformer. To the universal reformation of the world they stand
committed." Evangelical urgency thereafter infused the struggle against intemperance and slavery, which most reformers
identified as the chief sources of evil in American society.

Lyman Beecher, the influential Congregationalist evangelist from Connecticut, stated the new situation in a series of six
sermons delivered in 1825 and published the next year in
pamphlet form. "Intemperance is a national sin," he thun-
dered, "carrying destruction from the centre to every extrem-
ity of the empire, and calling upon the nation to array itself, *en
masse*, against it." The practice of drinking spirits should be
abolished, he argued, just as slavery had been uprooted in the

North. Theodore Dwight Weld, the prominent abolitionist, also tied the nation's destiny to its battle with alcohol. "All your country requires is, that you stop drinking ardent spirit," he declared in an 1832 oration. To those in the crowd who doubted their ability to control their appetite for liquor, Weld appealed to the logic of the revivals. "Didn't Jesus die on the cross?" he implored. "Can't you stop drinking?"

There was a close connection between the "new measures" adopted by the promoters of the revivals and the growing power of temperance reform. After Finney completed his celebrated Rochester revivals in 1831, a New York religious newspaper noted "that the Temperance Reformation and Revivals of Religion have a peculiarly intimate relation and bearing upon each other." Temperance not only fed off of the enthusiasm of the revivals but off of the methods of the revivalists. The ministers of the Second Great Awakening put a premium on organization and publicity. "What do the politicians do?" Finney asked. "They get up meetings, circulate handbills and pamphlets, blaze away in the newspapers, send coaches all over town with handbills . . . all to gain attention to their cause and their candidates." Christians in pursuit of a holier cause should do no less, he insisted. In seeking converts, religious organizations—the American Bible Society (1816), the American Sunday School Union (1824), and especially the American Tract Society (1825)—pioneered in the use of printed materials and voluntary associations to saturate Americans with vigorous moral appeals. The widespread distribution of printed matter and the fellowship of voluntary organizations became essential features of temperance reform in the 1820s.

Another new feature of the temperance movement linked to the revivals was the participation of women. Western evangelists, to the initial dismay of their Eastern brethren, invited

women to pray aloud in "promiscuous gatherings" of both
sexes and welcomed the influence of female converts on resistant family members. Women, although barred from leadership of temperance organizations, made up between 35 and 60
percent of the rank-and-file membership of local associations
and powerfully expressed the moral imperative of temperance
reform. Finally, the central feature of the revival—the public
act of individual conversion—was mirrored in the temperance lodges by the taking of the pledge, a public declaration
that one would abstain from intoxicating liquors.

In 1826 a group of reformers from evangelical backgrounds
founded the American Society for the Promotion of Temperance, known more familiarly as the American Temperance
Society (ATS). The ATS soon became the organizational hub
of the national temperance movement. Prompted by Lyman
Beecher's call for an organized effort to publicize the "statistics of temperance," the ATS illustrated the growth of temperance reform since the formation of the MSSI. Although still
led by prosperous laymen and clerics, the ATS defined temperance differently and adopted new methods to promote it.
In his influential sermons, Beecher argued that "the daily use
of ardent spirits, in any form, or in any degree, is intemperance." Abstinence from distilled liquor, rather than moderation in its use, became the benchmark of behavior for the
ATS. Members therefore pledged to refrain from drinking
spirits and to cut all ties to the liquor business.

Rather than applying the coercive force of law, the ATS relied on the tools of moral suasion. Fourteen of sixteen ATS di-
rectors were members of the American Tract Society, and the
new temperance society eagerly followed the practices of its
sister organization, flooding the country with millions of temperance pamphlets and sending paid itinerant speakers to follow up with personal testimony. One of the modern attributes

of the ATS, identified by the historian Robert Abzug, was its reliance on statistics to convey the danger to American society posed by intemperance. Temperance tracts combined Rush's pronouncements on the physical cost of drinking with doleful accounts of swelling populations in almshouses, insane asylums, and jails to drive home the individual and public damage wrought by drink. By extrapolating the figures from a single county, Weld argued that liquor had produced 300,000 drunkards, 10 percent of whom died annually, and accounted for half the nation's paupers, 80 percent of its incarcerated criminals, half of those committed to insane asylums, and nearly all its murderers. One temperance tract asserted that "where the slave trade opened *one* grave, hard drinking opens *three*." The ATS very clearly aimed its appeals at Americans attracted to reform and moral improvement. It hoped to alter behavior by means of organized persuasion rather than moral authority alone.

Although the purpose of the ATS was to target respectable moderate drinkers and influence middle-class behavior, by the 1830s its structure promoted a more broadly based, democratic temperance activism. The vision of the early ATS was coolly dismissive of drunkards. Justin Edwards, the society's key strategist, announced in 1826 his intention "to induce *those who are now temperate to continue so*. Then, as all who are *intemperate* will soon be dead, the earth will be eased of an amazing evil." Instead of dying, however, troubled drinkers began attending gatherings of local temperance bodies that were independent from the ATS or only loosely affiliated with the parent society. Grass-roots efforts to reform drunkards within a few years began to expand the reform scope of organized temperance.

Local initiative was possible because the national ATS functioned primarily as an information network. The national

body provided money, innovative propaganda through pamphlets and its newspaper, *The Journal of Humanity*, effective
speakers, and a commitment to moral suasion. Local associations gathered converts and generated action. Decentraliza-
tion also softened the elitism of the ATS. Unlike the MSSI, the
ATS allowed a proliferation of affiliated temperance clubs to
organize under its sponsorship. Therefore specialized temperance associations for artisans, blacks, young men, women, and
neighborhood and business groups joined county or city temperance societies. Diverse groups of Americans began to seek
the self-discipline, respect, and stable home lives promised by
temperance on their own terms rather than those prescribed
by religious and social elites. Women, who fulfilled their own
needs and those of their communities by involvement in
benevolent enterprises, were particularly active in spreading
petitions and raising money for local temperance societies. In
doing so they began to exert public influence in ways that
challenged their exclusion from formal political participation.
As the historian Lori Ginzberg has noted, "Virtually all
women who employed the language of moral change—those
active in charity work, moral reform, temperance, and aboli-
tion—moved casually into organizing for legislative action."

As temperance sentiment grew, the influence of the ATS
spilled into all regions of the nation and some of its principal
institutions. To help anchor the organization in local communities, the ATS selected active, ambitious leaders of local
reform efforts for membership in the society. In 1834 the
newly elected representatives of the ATS included 256
individuals residing in the Northeast, 74 Midwesterners, and
157 temperance workers from border states and the South. A
Congressional Temperance Society dedicated to voluntary organization and moral suasion was formed in 1833; by the next
year it had to move its annual meeting from the Senate cham-

ber to the larger House floor. By 1835, 1.5 million Americans in 8,000 affiliated associations were organized for temperance under the loose umbrella of the ATS. By succinctly diagnosing social ills and encouraging individual action to improve or even remake lives, temperance reform had grown into a major American social movement.

2

From Teetotalism to the Maine Laws

DURING A DECADE of tumultuous growth beginning in the early 1820s, American temperance reformers built a mass movement dedicated to self-discipline and moral improvement. Then, in the mid-1830s through the early 1840s, the temperance movement underwent a further important transformation. Three key developments were at the center of this transformation.

First, grass-roots enthusiasts pushed beyond the condemnation of distilled spirits and insisted that temperance advocates renounce fermented drinks as well. Total abstention from alcohol—teetotalism—soon became the standard goal of temperance reform, a position that put temperance organizations in much sharper opposition to traditional attitudes toward drink. Temperance no longer involved careful use of lighter alcoholic beverages; it required conversion to the use of cold water.

Second, the appearance of working-class and fraternal temperance societies, best represented by the Washingtonian movement, challenged the religious and middle-class dominance of temperance reform. This sparked a struggle for control of the movement, during which older temperance associations began to edge toward political action in the fight against alcohol.

The drift away from moral suasion toward legal coercion marked the third pivotal development during this crowded period. Tough-minded temperance reformers seeking fundamental alterations of American behavior soon dropped the voluntary ideal of temperance in favor of prohibition, the use of law to deny drinking Americans access to alcohol.

Scientific research, the influence of perfectionism, and the ambition of enthusiastic young men all played a hand in the triumph of teetotalism. Early temperance authorities had assumed that alcohol either was not present in fermented drinks such as wine, cider, or beer or had not acquired the damaging properties that distilling introduced. But by the 1820s chemists had established the presence of alcohol in fermented drinks. By the following decade, frustrated temperance backers had noted their intoxicating effects on backsliding drunkards and otherwise temperate men alike. In the 1840s expanded immigration from Germany would prompt the production of lager beer, a more commercially viable product than the bitter, fast-spoiling American brews, and a rapid increase of beer consumption; but this development was not yet powerful during the rise of teetotal sentiment. Instead the commitment to human perfection spread by the revivals led the sober-minded to seek greater self-discipline for themselves and sterner rules for keeping problem drinkers out of trouble. Too, wine drinking among elite temperance society members had begun to draw charges of hypocrisy from critics within and outside the movement. "There can be no difference between the guilt of one man, who indulges at the festive board or at a fashionable dinner party, in a revel over Madeira or Champaign, until Reason is dethroned, and that of another, who sits over his potations in a dram shop, until its considerate and merciful proprietor pitches him into the street," admitted United States Attorney General Benjamin Butler, a stout defender of the spirits-only proscription. The teetotal pledge, known as the "long pledge" to distinguish it from the "short pledge" to abstain from ardent spirits, first took hold in young men's and mechanics temperance societies in 1833 and 1834, prompted both by the idealism of youth and the wishes of employers who sponsored the clubs.

The rush of cold-water principles soon inundated the American Temperance Society. Prodded by Beecher, Edwards, and Edward Delavan, a wealthy sponsor of temperance enterprises, the ATS in 1836 adopted teetotalism, reorganized itself into the American Temperance Union (ATU), and briskly took the lead in the national fight against alcohol. Teetotalism cut off the possibility of half measures or compromise with drinkers or the liquor industry. It also provoked controversy within temperance circles. Uncomfortable debates over the legitimacy of communion wine strained goodwill. Harsh judgments were passed between some unbending teetotalers and those who preferred the short pledge. Some wealthy, prominent members of traditional temperance societies withdrew from the movement altogether. Teetotalism washed away the modest support for temperance previously shown by some Southern planters and reinforced the popular Southern image of temperance as another meddlesome, potentially disruptive New England reform craze. The ATU acknowledged the force of this impression and sought to counteract it by naming John Hartwell Cocke of Virginia as its president. Mainstream temperance had become a more radical reform, capable of bolder and more forthrightly political action.

The remarkable flowering of the Washingtonian movement in 1840 offered the further possibility that temperance reform could move beyond its foundations in evangelical Protestantism and middle-class respectability to become an authentic expression of working-class culture. According to the near-mythic account of its origins, Washingtonianism began with six Baltimore artisans who adjourned from a tavern to attend (and ridicule) a temperance meeting. Instead they found themselves converted to the doctrine of self-reform through teetotalism, and set out to reclaim other working-class drinkers. Naming their movement after the hero of American independence, the group enjoyed success in converting problem drinkers to teetotal principles, spread rapidly to other cities, and by 1841 had 200,000 adherents. Two years later the Washingtonian movement claimed more than one million converts pledged to teetotalism.

The roots of this extraordinary enthusiasm stretched back to the popularization of perfectionist thinking, local temperance initiatives to save drunkards, and, more concretely, the hard times and temptations produced by the economic depression of 1837 and the alcohol-soaked "hard cider" presidential campaign of 1840. The depression threw many skilled artisans out of work and threatened the security of others. Alcohol offered solace to the unemployed but drained scarce family resources. Some artisans turned to workingmen's mutual benefit associations for financial assistance, but the companionship in many such associations centered in tavern life. The temptation to engage in binge drinking presented by economic woes and male fraternity was furthered by the intense competition of the Harrison–Van Buren campaign of 1840, during which the "treating" of voters with drink reached epic proportions. Alarmed observers reported that "deluges of Brandy, gin, whiskey, and hard cider were poured down the throats of the undecided." The hopes of many skilled American workers were being washed away.

To the drunkard the Washingtonians offered acceptance and the chance for reform; to other working-class drinkers they offered inspiration, financial support, fellowship, and alternative sources of leisure. Washingtonianism attracted total abstainers as well as drinkers, middle-class clerks and employers as well as artisans. Briefly, mainstream temperance organizations pumped money and advice into Washingtonian associations. Nevertheless the new movement was plainly built to support working-class drinkers. Those who had feared for their own jobs better understood the connections between economic distress and intemperance and responded more forcefully to both dangers. After Washingtonians scoured the docks and alleys for drinkers to save, they furnished food, clothing, shelter, and even jobs to the troubled inebriates and their families.

The women's branches of the society, the Martha Washingtonians, were particularly attuned to the material consequences of intemperance for working-class families such as their own. Ruth Alexander's close study of the "Marthas" led her to conclude that "Washingtonian women were convinced that as wives and mothers they could not afford to remain silent while men, struggling to protect jobs, skills, and status in a changing economy, succumbed to the temporary pleasures of drink." When working-class Marthas encouraged young men to resist alcohol, the instability of their own fortunes added a poignancy that went beyond the solicitude of similar middle-class appeals. "Who can be independent," Marthas demanded of those who drank toasts to their status as free men, "when thousands of weeping mothers and sisters have followed their nearest and dearest relatives, broken-hearted, to a drunkard's grave?"

Washingtonian clubs offered drinking men the inspiration and excitement of a secularized revival to help them renounce the bottle, then provided a structure of male fraternity and amusement to replace tavern culture. Although prayers and clergymen were absent from most Washingtonian meetings, the ambience crackled with the same energy that had distinguished the revivals of the 1820s. Unlike other temperance societies that convened weekly or monthly, Washingtonian clubs met frequently—two, three, or four times each week—and exhibited the sustained level of excitement that evangelists had produced in protracted revivals. The centerpiece of the Washingtonian meeting was the "experience speech," in which a reformed drinker discussed frankly and vividly his own struggle with alcohol. Some reformed men, such as John Gough, who thrilled the great women's rights advocate Susan B. Anthony with his platform style, performed brilliantly enough to become professional temperance orators. But spontaneous, unpolished speeches from ordinary men were even more important in establishing fellowship and offering the possibility of self-improvement. With the suddenness and life-altering resolve that marked religious conversions during the revivals, drinkers embraced teetotalism at Washingtonian meetings.

Washingtonians provided amusements and activities to wean the pledge-takers from taverns. Their meetings were sometimes raucous affairs, with minstrel acts, comic songs, and jokes bandied about in the language of the streets. Some Washingtonian lodges were essentially taverns without alcohol. Outside the lodges, the movement sponsored temperance concerts, parades, picnics, and fairs. The explosive growth of the movement owed much to its willingness to provide a popular culture of temperance for working-class people.

As suddenly as it had appeared, however, Washingtonianism melted away. By 1843 hostility between the mainstream temperance organizations and the Washingtonians had become widespread. Supporters of middle-class respectability in the temperance movement considered Washingtonian enter-

tainment low and vulgar; many evangelical clerics found the
society of reformed drinkers irreligious. Similar criticisms
arose within Washingtonianism itself, as artisans intent on advancement and their middle-class allies moved to control
some locals. Dedicated Washingtonians fired back angrily.
The sniping between middle-class and working-class expressions of temperance helped dissolve the Washingtonians' loose
organizational structure. The pledge was the main unifying
feature of the movement: money and attempts at direction
had come from the now disaffected mainstream associations.
But the inevitable aftermath of the great harvest of converts in
1840–1841 set in during the 1842 and 1844 political campaigns
as thousands of pledge-takers slid back into intemperance.
The return of economic prosperity in 1843 also led some reformed men to fall away or shift their loyalties to labor unions.
Finally, the Washingtonian insistence on moral suasion began
to run up against the growing political activism of temperance
reformers. The reformed artisans among the Washingtonians
were extremely mistrustful of legal coercion—most of them
did not consider the state to be their protector—and clung to
the doctrine of voluntary self-reform. Without the resources
to discipline its wayward members, and with a commitment
to moral suasion after most other temperance reformers had
begun to doubt its utility, the Washingtonian movement scattered into fragments.

Many Washingtonians moved into similar but better organized fraternal temperance lodges. The biggest of them, the
Sons of Temperance, drew "respectable" Washingtonians
away at the time of its 1842 founding. The Sons surrounded
the temperance pledge with ritual, regalia, and fellowship of a
more orderly nature. When the head of the American Temperance Union, reflecting the evangelical suspicion of secret
societies left over from the anti-masonic movement of the

1830s, denounced fraternal orders as the "popery of temperance," the Sons obligingly eliminated some of their offensive rituals. To former Washingtonians, the Sons provided the security of a mutual benefit society, the camaraderie of a club, and what the historian Jed Dannenbaum termed "small scale communities" which offered a much-needed sense of belonging. By the end of the decade the Sons had enrolled more than 220,000 members in all sections of the country, and their women's auxiliary, the Daughters of Temperance, boasted 30,000 members. Other former Washingtonians who remained committed to the effort to reform drunkards continued their good works in smaller, more activist fraternal lodges such as the Good Samaritans and the Rechabites. Conventional temperance associations absorbed many of the remaining Washingtonians.

As Washingtonianism declined, temperance reform accelerated its movement away from moral suasion to embrace prohibition—the use of legal and political means to derail the liquor traffic and limit access to alcohol. By the 1840s voluntary organization and the power of moral appeals had made important inroads on American drinking patterns. The consumption of absolute alcohol by Americans aged fifteen and older had plunged from the 1830 figure of 7.1 gallons per capita to an average of 3.1 gallons in 1840. In 1845 consumption dropped to 1.8 gallons, the lowest average for the entire nineteenth century. Moreover, temperate habits had become the standard for middle-class behavior. Credit reports began to note the drinking practices of business proprietors. Even the unenthusiastic recognized the respectability conferred in middle-class society by temperance. In 1843 twenty-one-year-old Isaac Mickle of Camden, New Jersey, visited a stultifyingly dull temperance meeting. He confided to his diary that "my object in attending this meeting was not so much, I confess, to forward Temperance, as to administer an antidote" to rumors of improper behavior that threatened to damage his reputation. In forty years, abstention from alcohol had advanced from the curious enthusiasm of a few ascetics to a widely admired social grace.

Still, most temperance reformers felt that moral suasion had reached the limits of its influence. Even though drinking had become less of a fixture of American life, it had not been eradicated as perfectionism had predicted and as the turn to teetotalism had demanded. Many moderate drinkers criticized drunkenness but refused to consider their own tippling intemperate. Defiant pockets of more pronounced intemperance mocked reformers. Evidence from Cincinnati suggests that the Washingtonian revival influenced skilled workers, but hard-drinking laborers remained unaffected by the reform. The public intoxication that continued to accompany elections and holidays throughout the nation besmirched the image of democracy. In 1834 the Congressional Temperance Society pleaded for a show of sobriety during Fourth of July celebrations. "It cannot be necessary," their frustrated resolution stated, "that men shall exhibit themselves as drunkards and madmen, to show that they are worthy of freedom, and capable of self-government." Despite improvements, two decades of persistent moral suasion had not, in the eyes of some, removed the problem of alcohol from American society.

Social developments in the 1840s and 1850s increased the sense of urgency among advocates of temperance and other reforms. Beginning in the 1840s, immigration to the United States from Europe rose rapidly. Between 1845 and 1855 nearly 3 million immigrants, the vast majority from Ireland and Germany, arrived to start a new life in America. Many of them brought attitudes toward the use of alcohol that sharply conflicted with American temperance practices. Germans saw no incompatibility between drinking and family entertainment and further offended native Protestant sensibilities by enjoying their beer on Sundays. "Most of the people about here are Catholic German," a young Protestant acidly observed in 1855, "and they go to church at the Beer shop and go home drunk at night."

A more extensive array of complaints greeted the 1.5 million Irish newcomers. The great majority of Irish immigrants were young, penniless, male refugees from famine. Driven by familiar customs, their straitened circumstances in America, and loneliness, they drank whiskey, often to excess, in "bachelor groups." This culture of male drinking corresponded to early nineteenth-century American practices but alarmed middle-class natives in the 1840s who were already put off by the poverty and Catholicism of the Irish. Although a few Irish temperance societies that practiced moral suasion enjoyed modest success in America, and Germans were not noted for binge drinking, both Irish and German immigrants keenly resisted virtually all legal attempts to control drinking.

The crush of immigration was accompanied by a host of other indications that American society was growing more complex and unruly. Urban growth, particularly in the Midwest, accelerated as immigrants and rural migrants crowded into ill-prepared cities. Images of poverty, crime, violence, and immorality filled city newspapers. "No man is safe in the streets," reported the *Cincinnati Commercial*, "even *boys* sport their pistols! Strumpets have a wide range in the most prominent localities, and insult respectable ladies; vagabonds assail innocent men in the streets or go unmolested to brickbat or stone respectable houses." Gangs of toughs congregated in the cities, committing crimes, assaulting passersby, or fighting one another. Philadelphia, to cite one example, had an extensive network of youth gangs bearing such names as the Blood

Tubs, the Garroters, and the Killers. Riots against abolitionists, free blacks, Catholics, and immigrants were frequent
occurrences in the 1830s and 1840s. Reformers who had celebrated the impending perfection of American society in the
heady 1820s now faced an aggressive defense of slavery, out-
breaks of dueling and vigilante violence, and an increasingly
tense political atmosphere as the sectional crisis began to build.
On a wide array of fronts, reformers called for coercive, politically constructed measures to reach their goals. "Moral suasion
is moral balderdash," argued a writer in the *American Temperance Magazine* in 1852, bluntly explaining the need for prohibition statutes.

Traces of prohibitionist sentiment can be found from the
onset of organized temperance. Beecher's famous sermons of
1825, despite their emphasis on building popular temperance
opinion, identified as an ultimate goal "the banishment of ardent spirits from the list of lawful articles of commerce." The
logic of total abstinence, especially teetotalism, made moral
outlaws of the liquor industry. How could one attack drinking
as a vile and deadly disease and not attack the manufacture
and sale of alcohol? That was the position of Gerrit Smith, a
New York abolitionist and radical temperance reformer. In
1833 Smith successfully sponsored a resolution before a national temperance convention that condemned the liquor
trade as "morally wrong" and recommended that "local communities should be permitted by law to prohibit the said traffic within their respective jurisdictions." Since the awarding
of licenses to serve liquor at taverns and sell it at groceries had
from colonial days been a matter of public policy, the first attempts to restrict the liquor trade through political action focused on the sale, rather than the manufacture, of strong
drink.

As early as the 1830s, temperance advocates in New England tried to reduce the flow of distilled liquor in the towns and counties by blocking the issuance of licenses to sell spirits. The purpose was not to prevent all sale of liquor but rather to remove the seal of public sanction symbolized by licensing taverns and groceries. Temperance reformers hoped to combat what a Massachusetts district attorney called "the deceiving doctrine that ardent spirit is a benefit to the community—*a public good*." By forcing liquor sellers to carry on their business illegally, reformers intended to put the trade "on the level of brothel-keeping," a shameful and degrading practice.

The no-license campaigns of the 1830s borrowed from the methods of mass democratic politics to inject the temperance question into electoral affairs. The no-license movement in the bellwether state of Massachusetts illustrates the process by which temperance became politicized. Liquor-selling licenses were issued there by county commissioners upon the recommendations of town selectmen. During the early 1830s, temperance supporters at town meetings urged their selectmen to recommend no one to the commissioners for licensing, a tactic that by 1850 succeeded in drying up some entire counties. Commissioners, however, could ignore the recommendations of selectmen, so temperance reformers began to petition for local option—that is, direct popular referenda by which voters rather than officeholders determined the license question. Local option failed in the state legislature, but in 1835, for unrelated reasons, the county commissioners became subject to popular election. Thereafter county commissioner elections became battles between the supporters of license and no-license. Many cities and towns witnessed lively political fights over temperance. A coherent opposition to no-license began to emerge, consisting of those involved in the drink trade, defenders of tradition and community harmony, and those unsettled by the organized temperance legions with "their

national societies; their state societies; their county, half-
county, and town societies; their old men's, their young men's,
and their female associations—all operated for the same object, by the same power—the power of concerted action." The
issue of temperance in politics forced Americans to examine
the relative merits of individual liberty against the public
good, freedom versus improvement.

These divisions roughly paralleled those of the maturing
Second Party system, which had taken shape by 1834. At
that point, political opponents of Andrew Jackson had coalesced into the Whig party. The Whigs saw themselves as the
party of improvement, favoring government-sponsored roads,
banks, and other internal improvements. But the Whigs also
displayed a commitment to personal discipline, reason, and
progress which attracted many evangelicals, reformers, and
temperance advocates. Lyman Beecher, for instance, was a
Whig. Although some Whig leaders, most famously Henry
Clay, were prodigious drinkers, temperance sentiments were
more pronounced among the Whigs than was the case with
their Democratic rivals. Drink produced passion, Whigs argued, which in turn incapacitated reason and progress. A pro-
temperance editorial in the *New York Tribune*, an influential
Whig newspaper, denounced intemperance as "the complete
mastery of Man by a base appetite." In an 1842 address before
a local temperance club, the young Whig politician Abraham
Lincoln summarized the Whig philosophy: "Happy Day,
when, all appetites controled [sic], all passions subdued, *mind*,
all conquering *mind*, shall live and move the monarch of the
world."

Democrats, on the other hand, advanced themselves as the
party of liberty. Although Democrats such as Lewis Cass, the
secretary of war who ended the army's compulsory spirit ration, could be found in temperance ranks, most of those who

viewed temperance reform as an infringement of individual rights gave their allegiance to the party of Jackson. Thus a working-class woman in 1836 identified her husband's Democratic faith by saying, "He has always been Jackson and I don't think he has joined the Cold Water." An overwhelming number of Irish immigrants and most of the German newcomers also embraced the Democratic creed of liberty and popular rule. The fundamental outlooks that divided the two parties during the 1830s seemed to allow for the rise of temperance as a political issue.

It quickly became apparent, however, that prohibition, the coercive expression of temperance, cut across partisan lines in ways that made the two parties unwilling to face the issue squarely. Massachusetts again provides an example. Temperance advocates had turned from local prohibition contests to statewide policy, and in 1838 the state legislature enacted a modified prohibition statute known as the fifteen-gallon law. This measure tried to eliminate drinking in taverns and dramshops by allowing them to sell spirits for beverage purposes not by the glass but only in quantities of fifteen gallons or more. The Whig governor unenthusiastically signed the bill into law, knowing that he could not afford to oppose it but also aware that the state party would divide over the law's intrusiveness. As Massachusetts Whigs tore themselves apart over the merits of prohibition, Democrats emphasized the worthiness of temperate habits, ran a former president of the American Temperance Union for governor in 1840, and quietly signaled their disapproval of the law. A coalition of disgruntled Whigs and Democrats elected a Democratic governor, won a majority of legislative seats, and promptly repealed the fifteen-gallon law. There were many reasons for the Whig losses in 1840, but as the historian Ronald Formisano discovered, "among Whig politicos it rapidly be-

came accepted as gospel that the temperance law had caused
their party's defeat." A similar Mississippi law forbidding
liquor purchases of less than one gallon was also repealed in
short order. As the temperance movement increasingly pursued coercive measures to attack drinking in the 1840s, political parties tried to avoid prohibition as a partisan issue.

Prohibition became one of the factors that influenced the
decay of the Second Party system and the political realignment of the 1850s that featured the formation of the Republican party. After a scattering of no-license campaigns in the
late 1830s, the no-license movement flourished in the late
1840s—spreading from New England to Pennsylvania, New
York (where a local option statute in force between 1846 and
1848 dried up 728 out of 856 towns), and the Midwest. But the
movement found no stable support in the existing party system. Sometimes Whigs or Democrats supported no-license efforts; more often, independent political crusades drawing
Whig and Democratic temperance advocates out of their parties were necessary.

The difficulty in enforcing no-license laws further turned
prohibitionist-minded reformers against the parties and
elected officials. Most no-license statutes allowed the sale of alcohol for medical purposes. This exemption became the cover
for numerous fraudulent sales, but elected officials were slow
to crack down on abusers. In some spectacular incidents, public officials simply ignored no-license election results and continued to license liquor sales. Nearly everywhere, unlicensed
saloons were tolerated as courtroom tangles frustrated the
prosecution of license-law violators. Earnest temperance advocates, in concert with antislavery reformers and nativists,
began to view the parties as corrupt and unprincipled. A
widespread suspicion grew above the Mason-Dixon line that
the Slave Power, a supposed conspiracy of slaveholders and

their unscrupulous Northern defenders, was seizing hold of American political institutions. In the frightened imaginations of many Northerners, the Slave Power conspiracy explained the passage of the Fugitive Slave Law, the Kansas-Nebraska Act, and the proslavery Dred Scott decision of the Supreme Court. Alarmed temperance activists charged that an equivalent Rum Power, managed by the liquor industry and its political puppets, had thwarted the will of no-license voters. The alcohol-soaked campaign styles of both parties furthered the tawdry image. By the early 1850s, party compromises, backtracks, and evasions over the expansion of slavery, competing Protestant and Catholic demands on public school systems, immigrants, and temperance destroyed the Whig party and divided Democrats, causing Americans to search out new political loyalties. Novel political coalitions of dissatisfied temperance supporters began to demand unequivocal prohibition laws.

They found a model statute in the handiwork of Neal Dow, the mayor of Portland, Maine, who in 1851 forced a stringent statewide prohibition law through the Maine legislature. Dow was almost a caricature of the fanatical Yankee reformer: small in stature, vain, thrifty even though his tannery, banks, and real estate holdings made him wealthy, and utterly self-righteous. Despite his penchant for personal invective, Dow possessed political skills that, when linked with his indifference to party loyalty (he was nominally a Whig) and his supreme commitment to eradicating the blight of alcohol, made him a most effective anti-liquor politician. In 1851 he skillfully manipulated Democratic factionalism, Whig irresolution, and the temperance sympathies of a small Free Soil contingent (a third party devoted to keeping slavery out of new territories) to stitch together an impressive legislative majority for the country's strongest prohibition law.

The Maine Law was intended to close the loopholes that had undermined no-license efforts. It banned the manufacture and sale of alcoholic beverages by wholesalers and retailers. Liquor necessary for medicinal and mechanical purposes could be obtained only through bonded agents. The law made it far easier to seize illegal liquor and prosecute violators. Three voters, on evidence of an illegal sale, could obtain a search warrant to enter a building. If liquor was found and the owner could not prove that it was legally imported or was dispensed by a bonded agent, the alcohol could be destroyed. Fines for violations were stiffened, and third-time offenders were sent to prison. Logjams in the court were cleared by giving advantages to prosecutors, limiting the discretion of judges, and discouraging appeals by requiring bonds and imposing double fines on appeal convictions. The Maine Law had teeth, and Dow, enjoying his celebrity as the "Napoleon of temperance," took to the road to promote the passage of similar laws.

As party ties snapped asunder in the early 1850s, the Maine Law movement swept through the North. Between 1852 and 1855 twelve additional states—Massachusetts, Minnesota, Rhode Island, Vermont, Michigan, Connecticut, New York, Indiana, Delaware, Iowa, Nebraska, and New Hampshire—adopted Maine Laws. In Ohio, Pennsylvania, Illinois, and Wisconsin, attempts to enact prohibition created deep political divisions before falling short. Nearly everywhere, Whig and Democratic loyalties fractured over the politics of alcohol. "The temperance question is playing havoc in the old party lines," complained an Indiana Democrat. Divisions over the Maine Law in Massachusetts were so volatile that a Whig strategist counseled inaction, fearing that "taking ground either way would break up the party at the next election." As party professionals struggled to avoid confronting the issue of prohibition, political refugees in splinter parties—Free-Soilers, Anti-Nebraska coalitions, Know-Nothings—used their influence to force attention onto the issue. Only the South, focused rigidly on the sectional crisis over slavery and extraordinarily sensitive to the implications of coercive moral crusades championed by what one Virginian called a rabble of "Northern Yankees and Slavery agitators," uniformly rebuffed the Maine Law agitation.

Passed in an atmosphere of political crisis, the Maine Laws did not resolve the disagreement over the use of alcohol in the United States. Instead they provoked political and legal challenges, prompted episodes of violence, and furthered the dissolution of the established political system. Courts in Massachusetts (in 1854) and New York (in 1856) struck down the vital search-and-seizure provisions of the prohibition laws. Judicial decisions also quickly weakened Maine Laws in Minnesota, Michigan, and Indiana. Aroused by the passage of prohibition, liquor leagues began to appear in large cities to amass defense funds to challenge the laws. Prohibitionists, in turn, organized private groups to ensure the enforcement of the laws. The Carson League, the best known of these associations, maintained vigils outside suspected liquor dens and used informers, some of whom were paid, to ferret out violations of the law. Public policy had become private warfare.

The hostility of most Irish and German immigrants to prohibition further turned some temperance supporters, especially in rural areas, toward the anti-Catholic, nativist American (or Know-Nothing) party. After its sudden expansion in 1854, Know-Nothingism (so termed because of its origin as a secret order) made strong appeals to prohibitionists in several states and helped pass the Maine Laws of New York, New Hampshire, and Indiana. Violence flared as the ethnic dimensions of the conflict over liquor grew more apparent.

After the Know-Nothing mayor of Chicago announced in
1855 that saloons would be closed on Sundays, Germans took
to the streets in a disturbance known as the Lager Beer Riot.
The same year a band of militiamen commanded by Neal
Dow fired into a Portland crowd that Dow assumed to be
made up of Irish opponents of prohibition, killing one man.
Disorder, long the foe of the temperate, now seemed to be the
companion of prohibition.

The disabling of some prohibition laws, the controversy
surrounding the enforcement of others, and the dramatic in-
tensification of the sectional conflict quieted temperance activism as the nation slid toward civil war. The Republican
party, which grew from the debris of the shattered Second
Party system, attracted the support of many temperance advocates, but the managers of the new party quickly pushed aside
divisive issues like prohibition and nativism to focus on the extension of slavery. By 1860, the year that Republican candidate
Abraham Lincoln gained the presidency, four of the Maine
Law states had repealed prohibition. The law was minimally
enforced or ignored in most of the others as the nation moved
toward its great conflict.

After several decades of spectacular growth as a social
movement, temperance reform had seemingly reached the
limits of its influence. For the remainder of the century, party
strategists would try to muzzle temperance reform and subor-
dinate it to partisan ends. Many moderate temperance supporters, concluding that prohibition was an ill-timed response
to a unique period of political crisis, cooled their enthusiasm
for large-scale legal solutions to the drink problem. After
achieving the status of a mainstream reform in the first half of
the nineteenth century, the continued drive for prohibition in
the post–Civil War years became a movement of outsiders.

3

A Movement of Outsiders

THE UNITED STATES grew into a modern industrial nation in the second half of the nineteenth century, but as their society matured most Americans lost the reforming zeal that had distinguished the years before the Civil War. The huge cost of the war and the disappointing outcome of Reconstruction inhibited the spread of perfectionist expectations. The antebellum empire of reform quietly disintegrated. Enormous energy infused the industrial and urban growth of Gilded Age America, but regulatory attempts to direct social change faded in the face of the traditional American reliance on market forces and deference to local customs. Alcohol was subject to the same combination of haphazard regulation and surrender to localism that characterized American society as a whole during these restless years.

The wave of temperance enthusiasm that surged through the first half of the nineteenth century reached its crest in the 1850s, then began to ebb. The movement's success at driving down average alcohol consumption from the excess of the 1820s partially explains the drop in fervor; between 1850 and 1900, average consumption of pure alcohol wavered between 1.8 and 2.1 gallons. The impending crisis of the Union and the shattering impact of the Civil War also diverted attention from temperance reform. But the most powerful institutional obstruction to continued temperance agitation was the political system itself. The volatility of the liquor issue, revealed by the Maine Law campaigns of the 1850s and their political residue after the war, generated strong resistance to prohibition within the Democratic and Republican parties of the late nineteenth century. Politicians discovered that alcohol created disorder in politics as well as in the lives of troubled drinkers.

From the 1850s until the 1870s, arguments over sectionalism, war, and Reconstruction brought parties to collapse or divided them into tangled, angry factions. For the remainder of the century, a period dubbed the Third Party system by modern scholars, both Democrats and Republicans emphasized stability, party loyalty, and intricate organization. Gilded Age politics was marked by high voter turnout, competitive elections, strong party identification, and the avoidance of internally divisive issues. The cavalcade of bland, humdrum presidents following Lincoln and preceding Theodore Roosevelt symbolizes the triumph of organizational politics over exciting or challenging issues in the late nineteenth century. Party needs determined the posture of elected officials; party officials craved unity, not disruption.

Although personal temperance was still a widely respected virtue, the advocacy of prohibitory legislation increasingly fell to dissident factions within the dominant parties or those outside the structure of the two parties altogether. Disenchanted temperance activists who left the major parties to launch the Prohibition party in 1869 represented one such group. The other was made up of American women: ineligible to vote and thereby excluded from direct influence in the party system; unprotected by the legal system that repealed or failed to enforce restrictive liquor laws; and persuaded by the ideology of domesticity and, in many cases, the experience of their own lives that alcohol posed an immediate and implacable threat to their families. Beginning in December 1873 clusters of middle-class women in small towns periodically marched through the streets of their communities, entered saloons or ringed them with praying women, and closed them down. For the next seven months this grass-roots direct-action campaign spread through the Midwest, the mid-Atlantic region, and the Pacific coast. By the end of 1874 the most dynamic and influential women's organization of the nineteenth century, the Woman's Christian Temperance Union, was formed. Led after 1879 by the energetic and charismatic Frances Willard, the WCTU forced temperance reform and eventually prohibition back onto the political agenda.

The temperance movement, already slowed by the Maine Law controversies of the 1850s, suffered further setbacks during the Civil War. By 1865 only five states retained their prohibition laws as patriotic commitments crowded out temperance zeal. Wartime policy more directly undercut temperance efforts, as in the case of the 1862 Internal Revenue Act. This measure, part of the expanded system of taxes generated to finance the war, taxed distilled and malt liquors and required that retailers of alcoholic drinks purchase a federal license. Temperance advocates complained that the law restored legitimacy to a disgraced trade and rendered the United States a partner in the unholy commerce. In an unsuccessful effort to eliminate federal licensing of liquor, Massachusetts senator Henry Wilson argued that "the Federal Government ought not to derive a revenue from the retail of intoxicating drinks." Wartime expediency overshadowed temperance objections, however, and until the onset of national prohibition, federal, state, and local government relied on the liquor trade for much of its tax revenue.

Temperance enthusiasts also charged that military life had

reignited the culture of male drinking. The army restored its spirits ration early in the war (the Confederacy also supplied liquor to its troops), and visitors to the camps reported that intemperance was rife among officers and even chaplains, let alone the men in the ranks. Many families dreaded the exposure of their young men to the snares of drinking, gambling, and prostitution in camp as greatly as they feared the dangers of combat. Countermeasures were swiftly taken by the temperate. The American Temperance Union, followed later by the Union Reform Association, deluged the Union forces with tracts urging total abstinence. Temperance-minded soldiers grouped together in military units. Neal Dow formed a temperance regiment and maintained the cold-water discipline among his troops as he rose to the rank of general. Ohio's Rutherford B. Hayes assured his anxious mother in 1861 that his regiment was "strictly a temperance camp." Nevertheless the temptations and disorderliness that accompanied military experience help explain the heightened concern for the fate of young men that distinguished postwar temperance rhetoric.

Beyond the possibilities of a revived male drinking culture introduced by the war, the forces of temperance encountered a better organized and more politically active liquor industry in the immediate aftermath of the conflict. The new federal tax on beer prompted the organization of the United States Brewers' Association in 1862, a trade group that negotiated with the government over the particulars of the excise. As early as 1867 a USBA congress threatened to act politically against temperance supporters. But the national associations of brewers and distillers would spend more time in the late nineteenth century quarreling with each other than effectively guiding resistance to prohibition initiatives. More important in the political struggles that directly followed the war were local and state liquor dealers associations, which coalesced to fight the enforcement of remaining prohibition and no-license statutes.

At the conclusion of the Civil War in 1865, temperance advocates acted to revitalize their flagging movement. Another national temperance convention replaced the weakened ATU with a new national organization, the National Temperance Society and Publication House. At the same time fraternal temperance associations, most notably the Independent Order of Good Templars, experienced rapid growth. Between 1865 and 1869, membership in the Templars soared from 60,000 to 400,000. Both the National Temperance Society and the Templars demanded a renewed commitment to prohibition. Spurred by local activists and in tune with the short-term wave of government activism across the United States in the late 1860s, Massachusetts in 1865 created a state constabulary to enforce the long-dormant prohibition law of 1855. Squads of constables, many of them Union veterans, in 1867 seized roughly 100,000 gallons of spirits in Boston's Suffolk County. That same year a state police force was formed in Maine to enforce prohibition. Also in 1867, Pennsylvania's legislature enacted a law banning Sunday sales of liquor and empowering lawmen to close down violators. Maryland and New York also took fresh steps to stop Sunday liquor sales. "Liquor dealers were the most oppressed people in this country," complained representatives of the trade in Philadelphia. Prohibition again appeared to be on the march.

But the political opposition to stringent liquor laws outmuscled the prohibitionists. Massachusetts liquor dealers organized a pressure group called the Personal Liberty League and worked to elect legislative candidates committed to the repeal of prohibition. Although a minority of the dominant state Republicans favored the strict laws, former governor

John Andrew was a vocal critic of prohibition, and many others in the GOP questioned the need for the expanded police force. Most important, Republicans refused to make prohibition a party issue. Instead, candidates were left to stake out individual positions on the liquor question. Voters in the 1867 election clearly demonstrated the unpopularity of the renewed prohibition measures in the Bay State. Pro-license Republicans and Democrats were swept into office, and prohibition in Massachusetts was temporarily repealed (permanent repeal came in 1875).

In Pittsburgh, German liquor dealers gathered "friends of social liberty" into a self-styled Reform Society dedicated to enfeebling license restrictions. Germans in Kansas organized in 1867 to blunt temperance advances, and in Iowa an independent political movement called the People's party formed to battle prohibitionists. When the mayor of Chicago dared to enforce the state Sunday-closing law in 1872, Irish and German Chicagoans launched their own People's party and drove him from office. Prohibition had become the political equivalent of nitroglycerin, too unstable and explosive an issue to be safely handled.

Prohibition was particularly troubling for Republicans in the late 1860s and early 1870s. Most Americans who were inclined to support anti-liquor laws were Republicans. They celebrated the GOP as the savior of the Union, the party of progress, and, because of its role in the destruction of slavery, the political champion of moral ideas. Republicans encouraged the exercise of governmental power to promote industrial growth, improve public schools, and advance the public good. Republican partisans considered the Democratic party negative and reactionary, a drag on progress. "Which party," demanded a Republican editor in 1875, "depends upon the ignorance and prejudice of the voters? Which is strongest in the slums of great cities, and in rural parts of the Union where there are fewest schools?" It was, of course, the Democrats.

Yet controversies over temperance laws tended to strengthen Democrats and hurt Republicans. Although many Democrats practiced personal temperance and even supported some regulation of the liquor industry, the party as a whole expressed its commitment to "personal liberty" in the matter of drinking. "Why do you allow the dyspeptic Radicalism of Boston to tell you what to drink, and when and how you must behave on Sunday?" asked a New York Democratic congressman in 1867. Prohibition not only endangered the preferences and customs of drinkers, including Protestant Germans who normally voted Republican, it also provoked among Democrats the old Jacksonian fear of arbitrary power. The 1870 platform of the Indiana Democratic party denounced Republican intentions "to regulate the moral ideas, appetites, or innocent amusements of the people by legislation." By challenging anti-liquor laws, Democrats in the mid-1870s won elections in Indiana, Wisconsin, Michigan, Pennsylvania, and Massachusetts. In the highly competitive politics of the Third Party system, issues that energized voters in one party and alienated small groups in the opposition party, enough to keep them from voting or even cause them to "scratch" their ballots and cross party lines, were often decisive in elections. Alcohol regulation became such an issue in the decade following the Civil War.

Already hampered by the difficulties of Reconstruction, the Republican party began to distance itself from prohibition. The awkwardness with which some party officials disengaged from the temperance embrace alarmed anti-liquor Republicans. In Pennsylvania, for instance, delegates to an 1867 temperance convention were delighted to hear Republican governor John W. Geary deliver the keynote address. Geary

announced that he was a teetotaler and proudly declared that
his election campaign "was conducted on temperance principles, strict and pure." No previous Pennsylvania governor had
linked himself so closely to the temperance movement. But in
the 1869 election campaign, Geary maintained a studied silence on the subject of alcohol and never again attended a
temperance conference. Some prohibitionist Republicans felt
"deceived" and "betrayed" by Geary. Dry Republicans received a further shock in 1872 when the national party
approved a platform plank that discouraged laws "for the purpose of removing evils, by interference with rights not
surrendered by the people to either the state or national government." Although the language of the statement was ambiguous, the fact that it was drafted by the editor of the *Illinois
Staats Zeitung*, one of the Midwest's chief German newspapers, made the party's intentions clear: in a gesture to its German constituency, the Republican party was backing away
from anti-liquor legislation. By the late 1870s only the states
forming the dry stronghold of northern New England—Vermont, New Hampshire, and Maine—retained their 1850s
prohibition laws.

Beginning in the early 1870s, cautious politicians returned
liquor regulation to local jurisdictions and individual initiative, most commonly by revisions of old license laws. Illinois
and Wisconsin, for example, in 1872 gave village, town, and
city officials the authority to license liquor sales. Between 1872
and 1875 Pennsylvania legislators turned the licensing decision over to local city and county voters with the passage of a
local-option bill. Some states, such as Kansas, required that
petitions from the community in question accompany license
applications. In other cases, seemingly stringent liquor legislation relied on individual citizens for enforcement. Nearly a
dozen states passed laws similar to the Illinois Dramshop Act

of 1872, which barred liquor sales to minors and drunkards and held liquor sellers financially liable for injuries and damage caused by their intoxicated customers. But these civil damage laws required injured parties to initiate lawsuits to bring the statutes into play—individuals rather than the state were left to implement the law. An especially egregious example of this retreat from government activism came in Ohio, where, following passage of a strong civil damage law in 1870, state officials slowed their enforcement of Ohio's strict no-license constitutional requirement and left liquor-law violators and their outraged opponents to fight it out in court.

The circumspection with which Republican party officials approached the liquor question forced some temperance advocates to push for a new political party dedicated to the cause of prohibition. In the spring of 1869 the Grand Lodge of the Good Templars proposed that a mass convention of teetotaler organizations meet to arrange "district political action for temperance." Gathering in Chicago later that year, anti-liquor activists observed that "the existing parties are hopelessly unwilling to adopt an adequate policy on this question," and therefore launched the Prohibition party to carry on the war against drink unfettered by the conflicting interests of the mass-constituency parties. In 1872 the party nominated its first presidential ticket.

The Prohibition party appealed to the memory of antebellum reform and the founding spirit of the Republican party— among its state candidates in 1870 were the Massachusetts abolitionist Wendell Phillips and James Black, a founder of the Republican party in Pennsylvania. But in the intense partisan atmosphere of the late nineteenth century, only a few thousand temperance voters were willing to abandon their party affiliation to take up the Prohibition banner. Even the great surge in Prohibition support in the presidential elections

of 1884 through 1892—when the Prohibition party vote
leaped from about 10,000 to 150,000 (1884), then 250,000
(1888), and finally 271,000 (1892)—never represented more
than 2.2 percent of the total votes cast. Most temperance-
minded Republicans, and pockets of temperance Democrats,
remained part of prohibitionist factions in their state and local
party organizations. Using grass-roots pressure, they pushed
their leaders to back stronger anti-liquor measures and, when
rebuffed, occasionally communicated their displeasure by sitting out elections or joining with third-party fusion movements to support candidates who favored more aggressive dry
proposals. Their influence grew stronger, even decisive in
some states, by the 1880s, but throughout the Gilded Age active support for prohibition remained a movement on the
margins of power, resisted by the mainstream political structure. This was especially true of the women's movement to
close down saloons.

Women occupied a paradoxical position in the American temperance movement of the mid-nineteenth century. On the one
hand, the dedication and enthusiasm of female volunteers
were critical assets in building temperance into a mass movement. But as the movement grew powerful enough to advance
political solutions to the problems of intemperance, women
found themselves shunted to the margins. Women circulated
petitions and lobbied legislators in support of prohibition
laws, but they lacked the central tool of pressure politics—the
vote. Women's voices were also muffled within temperance
organizations. In 1853 a so-called "World's Temperance Convention" in New York City split rancorously over the issue of
women's participation, prompting the organization of a rival
"Whole World's" convention that seated blacks and women.
Ultimately the "World's" convention tacitly allowed female

delegates to remain seated but conformed to the "common usages of society" and banned women from addressing the convention. It was, in the resolution of Ohio temperance women, "a most daring and insulting outrage upon all *woman kind*."

The Maine Law campaigns of the 1850s therefore made plain a central contradiction in temperance reform to that point: temperance reform needed the support of women to succeed, yet women were not allowed to exercise leadership or direction over the movement. Senator Theodore Frelinghuysen underlined the operating assumptions of antebellum temperance reform when he reminded his office-holding colleagues that "we *must* have the benefit of female philanthropy" to defeat alcohol. Late-nineteenth-century women, however, refused to define temperance activism as philanthropy; for them it was the urgent public business of "home protection."

The social and cultural context of drinking in Victorian America placed women squarely in the center of the fight against alcohol. First of all, drinking itself was now increasingly defined as a male activity. Researchers have found that for all ethnic groups except the Irish, men in this period drank far more than did women. For native-born, middle-class women, the lessons of temperance and the Victorian code of propriety both counseled against frequent tippling. This does not mean that middle-class American women were, as a class, teetotalers. Many such women consumed alcohol in the form of medicine or with meals as aids to digestion. In the early 1870s Frances Willard, soon to become the chief symbol of female temperance, drank wine while traveling in Europe and took a daily medicinal glass of beer with dinner during a rocky tenure as a college dean. Patent medicines and tonics that were popular with women often were laced with alcohol. When most middle-class women drank, however, it was at home or in culturally sanctioned contexts. Male drinking, on the other hand, increasingly became linked to the saloon, an institution tainted with images of illegality and contempt for family values.

The saloon, a term that became popular in the late 1850s to describe a retail liquor establishment that served drinks by the glass, became a symbol for the dangerous aspects of the male drinking culture. Although women (and even children) patronized saloons, they usually did so to make carry-out purchases in the afternoon at back or side doors. The inside of the saloon was a masculine domain. There men congregated outside the family circle and drank—pleasantly much of the time, but often improvidently and sometimes morbidly. The proliferation of unlicensed saloons—known as blind pigs—and the operation of illegal "kitchen barrooms," in which immigrant and working-class women sold beer and whiskey inside their tenement dwellings, lent an unwholesome air to the business.

The anti-liquor policies of a handful of labor organizations furthered the impression that saloons endangered steady habits and stable lives. The Knights of Labor, a national union which attracted artisans and reformers, excluded liquor dealers from membership. Prompted by a desire to build a cohesive working-class culture apart from saloons, and angered by the ties between local saloons and the anti-labor Republican machine in Denver, the Knights of Labor in that Colorado city even formed a brief political alliance with the Prohibition party in 1886. Members of the railway brotherhoods, whose taxing jobs required precision and alertness, were sworn to abstain from alcohol. Beyond the brutality of drunken husbands and fathers, or the damage done by squandered wages or alcohol-induced accidents, the very fact that many American men spent time away from home drinking caused unease in an age that lavished sentimental affection on the ideals of home and family.

Women were culturally positioned to feel such threats most keenly. The ideals of domesticity already encouraged women to act as moral guardians for their families and to tutor their children in the duties of virtuous citizenship. Antebellum women had identified drunkenness as an affront to middle-class respectability and working-class survival, a threat to the health and harmony of families, and a peril awaiting every boy as he grew to manhood. After 1850, Victorian sentimentality and the practices of the saloon trade magnified this fear. Motherhood in the mid-nineteenth century shifted from a duty to a sacrament of sorts, as romantic notions of the special relationship between mothers and their children flooded popular culture.

At the same time a maudlin popular temperance literature, which emphasized the threat of saloon culture to the middle-class family, became influential. Its masterpiece was Timothy Shay Arthur's *Ten Nights in a Barroom*, which appeared at the height of the Maine Law movement. This melodrama chronicled the financial, moral, and emotional destruction of Joe Morgan and his family after his enslavement by the alcoholic wares of the heartless saloonkeeper Simon Slade. When Morgan's daughter comes to fetch him home, Slade throws a glass that kills the girl. Later Slade dies at the hands of his own drunken son. As the historian Norman Clark points out, Arthur's tale emphasized that the drink trade was as unnaturally cruel and destructive to family life as slavery had been portrayed in the popular abolitionist novel *Uncle Tom's Cabin*. When *Ten Nights* was adapted for the stage, during its long run American audiences already familiar with the villainous symbol of slavery, Simon Legree, learned to hiss as well at the soul-wrecking vendor of intemperance, Simon Slade.

Meanwhile the commercial expansion of the retail liquor business in the late nineteenth century helped make saloons more visible offenders of Victorian sensibilities. Between 1864 and 1873 the number of retail liquor outlets in the United States increased annually by 17.1 percent, easily outdistancing the 2.6 percent annual population growth rate. Liquor-selling drugstores, groceries, and especially saloons became far more commonplace features of American communities. According to the historian Jack Blocker, in 1864 there was one retail liquor dealer for every 432 Americans; in 1873 this ratio dropped to one dealer for every 210 people. Almost 205,000 dealers paid the federal excise tax in the latter year. Americans intent on slaking an alcoholic thirst found it easier than ever to buy a drink.

In an increasingly competitive industry, saloonkeepers attracted customers with special offers and inducements that encouraged heavy drinking. Some saloons provided a free lunch with the purchase of a drink. Bartenders built up a clientele by starting each day's business with a free round; they invited their patrons to treat one another; and, in a widely condemned practice, many of them slipped free liquor to underage customers to acquaint the young ones with the taste.

The appearance and atmosphere of late-nineteenth-century saloons as centers of a rough masculine society further antagonized middle-class women. Outside of ethnic bars and clubs that invited family groups, most American saloons catered to men. Many saloons advertised cigars as well as liquor on their windows; their floors were usually sprinkled with poorly aimed tobacco juice. Paintings of female nudes gave a hint of illicit sexuality to even the best hotel bars. Among the low-grade places, curtained "wine rooms," upstairs bedrooms, and the presence of prostitutes confirmed to worried observers the connection between alcohol and sexual transgression. By the

early twentieth century the contradictory images of motherhood and barroom culture had grown so powerful that the
presiding officer of the Illinois senate declared that no legisla-
tor could support open saloons on Sunday "without violating
the inheritance which he had from his mother."

The social and cultural climate of the United States thus infused a special intensity into the temperance convictions of
middle-class women at the same moment that temperance reform was absorbed into politics, where women could exercise
only indirect influence. Rather than rely on men's willingness
to pass and enforce stringent liquor laws, as early as the 1850s
some women acted boldly to challenge their exclusion from
public life. For the most radical among them, this meant demanding woman suffrage in addition to prohibition. After
her attempt to address a Sons of Temperance meeting in 1852
had been denied—with the chilly rebuke that "the ladies had
been invited to listen and not take part in the proceedings"—
Susan B. Anthony began her journey from temperance reform
to the suffrage movement by helping found the New York
State Women's Temperance Society. The NYSWTS enrolled
two thousand members before breaking apart over the
women's rights agenda proposed by Anthony and Elizabeth
Cady Stanton. In 1853 Stanton appealed to the New York
state legislature to enact prohibition and a liberalized divorce
law that would allow women to separate themselves from
intemperate husbands. Throughout the country, women
showed their dissatisfaction with the male-dominated temperance lodges by streaming into the Independent Order of Good
Templars, which offered women membership on equal foot-
ing with men. The Maine Law drive had pushed women to
act more aggressively to defend their place in temperance reform.

The failure of politics represented by the repeal, weaken-

ing, or defeat of prohibition laws that quickly followed the
Maine Law campaigns produced surprising action on the part
of respectable middle-class women in scattered communities
across the country. Frustrated by court decisions dismantling
saloon restrictions, and by the timidity or refusal of elected officials to enforce laws, women in small towns banded together
and "enforced laws of their own making"—they took up axes
and destroyed the liquor supply in local saloons. These vigilante attacks occurred between 1853 and 1859 in dozens of
towns in Illinois, Ohio, Indiana, Michigan, Massachusetts, and
other Northern states; immediately after the Civil War, several more raids occurred. Rather than condemn the women,
many of whom were from prominent families, local opinion
supported the vigilantes. Crowds cheered the destruction of
liquor, men disarmed angry saloonkeepers, juries acquitted
the women of criminal charges, and newspapers glorified
their exploits. Abraham Lincoln, who defended a group of
saloon-destroying women from Marion, Illinois, in 1854, com-
pared their actions to those of the patriots at the Boston Tea
Party. At least in some small American towns, people sympa-
thized with women's frustration at the failure of the legal system to suppress the drink trade and supported their violent
display of domesticity. These scattered episodes in the 1850s
foreshadowed the much grander and more influential
Women's Crusade of 1873–1874, when women in thirty-one
states marched through the streets to close down saloons.

The Women's Crusade was a short, sharp demonstration of
the intense threat that middle-class women felt from the expansion of the retail liquor industry in the early 1870s and the
powerlessness they experienced in the face of government inaction to curb the drink trade. The spark that ignited this extraordinary outburst of direct-action protest was struck in
December 1873 by Dio Lewis, a holdover from the antebellum

reform era. Lewis was a traveling lecturer and reform enthu-
siast. One of his stock speeches, "The Duty of Christian
Women in the Temperance Work," recalled how in the 1830s
his mother had managed to close the four saloons in her small
New York town by leading a group of singing, praying
women into the barrooms and convincing their owners to
cease operations. The women had been motivated, in alternate
versions of the tale, either by domestic abuse on the part of a
drinking husband or by an episode in which thirteen boys
were lured into the liquor dens by saloonkeepers.

Lewis had delivered this talk hundreds of times over
twenty years and claimed to have launched peaceful sieges of
saloons in a handful of towns during the 1850s. He stressed
the vulnerability of families to the liquor trade and encouraged a mode of feminine protest more in keeping with domestic ideals than had been exhibited in the more publicized
hatchet-wielding affrays of the 1850s. Nevertheless, the talk
had resulted in no significant action since 1858. Then suddenly, at the end of 1873, appearances by Lewis in Fredonia
and Jamestown in western New York and in the southern
Ohio towns of Hillsboro and Washington Court House
prompted local women to march on saloons and urge liquor
sellers to destroy their stock. Through the winter and into the
spring of 1874, propelled by newspaper coverage, word of
mouth, and visitations from Crusader veterans, the Women's
Crusade spread to every section of the country except the deep
South, involving 911 communities and engaging the efforts of
more than 57,000 and as many as 143,000 women before the
grass-roots enthusiasm was played out. More than one-third
of the Crusades took place in Ohio, but Indiana, Illinois,
Michigan, and New York each experienced at least sixty Crusades. Lewis did not create this decentralized mass movement,
he simply gave it the opportunity to discover itself.

The Women's Crusade was the combustible product of the large retail liquor trade, the postwar upsurge in middle-class male drinking, government hesitancy to enforce restrictive liquor regulations, and women's heightened concern for the safety of their families—all of which by 1873 reached a critical point. Jack Blocker's careful reconstruction of the Crusade in Washington Court House, Ohio, reveals that small towns, the most common locations for Crusade activity, were particularly susceptible to these pressures.

Washington Court House was a small market center, six blocks long and four blocks wide, in the flat farm country between Cincinnati and Columbus. Only two thousand people lived there, but the town contained eleven saloons and three drugstores that sold liquor. These places drew customers from the surrounding countryside, including farmers and those attending to legal business at the county seat, in addition to town residents. Public drinking within the county was thus concentrated into a very small space, so that townspeople found it impossible to avoid the noise, rowdiness, and violence that accompanied saloon drinking. Drunken toughs sometimes went out of their way to insult townspeople, making crude remarks on the street, ambushing travelers at the nearby covered bridge, and, in the case of one irreligious reveler, hurling brickbats and stones through the windows of a local church during services. Alcohol also seemed to desecrate private life. Local newspapers regularly carried stories of drunken men beating or mistreating their wives and children.

Despite sidewalk encounters with vulgar men and the disruption of worship, local women most feared the impact of saloons on their own male family members. Most of the problem drinkers Blocker identified in Washington Court House were men living outside the immediate supervision of their families: either bachelors or young adults boarding away from their parents. On the other hand, the average Crusader was a prosperous woman in her thirties or forties, married or widowed, and devoted to her family. In many cases these women were personally acquainted with male intemperance. The leader of the Crusade in neighboring Hillsboro, Eliza Thompson, was the daughter of a former governor but also the mother of a promising son who drank himself out of jobs as a minister and a teacher, was confined for a time to an inebriate asylum, and died at the age of thirty. The husbands and sons of several Washington Court House Crusaders had been arrested for drunkenness, often more than once.

Women were doubly angered: by their inability to restrain young men living outside the home, and by the fact that, according to state and local statutes, there should be no saloons in Washington Court House at all. State law barred the sale of spirits by the glass, and a town ordinance outlawed the sale of beer, ale, and porter. Periodic attempts to enforce the laws, however, had met resistance and disturbed political alignments, so the state of Ohio, in a pattern shared across the nation in the early 1870s, left it up to women themselves to challenge liquor-law violations by initiating civil damage suits against saloonkeepers and druggists. Few women had the money or the legal resources to pursue such suits. Desperate to protect themselves and their families, resentful of a political system that forced them to rely on men to guard their interests and offered no remedy when laws were ignored, women in Washington Court House were primed for action when Dio Lewis came to town.

Although tactics varied from place to place, most Crusaders insisted that religious duty and family devotion compelled them to act. In that spirit of womanly concern, they strove to comport themselves according to the dictates of the Christian "law of love." In Washington Court House, women carried an appeal to saloonkeepers, asking them "to desist from this ruinous traffic, that our husbands, brothers, and especially our sons, be no longer exposed to this terrible temptation, and that we may no longer see them led into those paths which go down to sin and bring both soul and body to destruction." Druggists and doctors were asked not to dispense alcohol for beverage purposes. As churches filled with praying male supporters tolled their bells, groups of forty to seventy-five women slowly marched to saloons, asked to be admitted, and then prayed inside the saloon or, if rebuffed, on the sidewalk outside, usually before a crowd of curious or hostile men. Women marched in about half the communities that experienced Crusade activity. In many locales women also handed out total abstinence pledges to men in the community and petitioned officeholders to enforce existing laws. In Washington Court House the marches and petitions were accompanied by a barrage of civil damage lawsuits filed by male supporters of the Crusade.

Crusaders sometimes modulated the law of love in order to apply extra pressure to holdouts among saloonkeepers. After the saloons and drugstores within Washington Court House surrendered to the women, determined Crusaders trained locomotive lights onto the property of a defiant beer-garden owner in the county outside town and noted the names of his customers. Despite their meek demeanor, women acted, in the words of a Cleveland Crusader, "to show the traffic in ardent spirits to be disgraceful and wicked, to make it hazardous, to make it unprofitable." Crusaders became involved in political campaigns—mostly no-license elections—in about 19 percent of the cases, but usually this was the result of unsuccessful direct-action tactics. In California, for instance, after the utter failure of saloon marches, women crusaders in San Jose and Alameda massed on election day to serve food and encourage voters to support no-license. In both cases, women were threatened and eventually attacked by crowds of jeering men, emboldened by free election-day beer, and pro-license forces triumphed.

The Women's Crusade demonstrated the depth of temperance conviction in many communities, but it also exhibited the limited power of women acting alone in the public sphere. Crusades were most successful in small towns where relatively large numbers of Crusaders—Washington Court House had 150 women participants—with strong local support could apply maximum pressure on a small number of liquor retailers. Support networks were vitally important, for the opposition to the Crusades, although often courteous, was determined and sometimes loud and threatening. The sheer size of large cities and the presence there of better-organized resistance from liquor dealers, drinkers, and opponents of female activism hampered Crusaders in Chicago, Cleveland, Cincinnati, Pittsburgh, and other urban centers. In settlements of every size, saloon operators and patrons staged counter-demonstrations, drowned out prayers with music and pot-banging, crowded the sidewalks with obstructions, and showered Crusaders with beer, paint, rotten eggs, excrement, stones, and chunks of wood. Although the Crusaders usually steered clear of nativist appeals, many Germans saw the Crusade as an unwarranted assault on their cultural traditions and stoutly resisted its overtures.

In the end, however, the Women's Crusade was undermined by its own emphasis on women's direct action. Crusaders argued that the lack of public authority left them without alternatives to street protests. "Why deny to those who have sinned least and suffered most the use of the only weapons left them," pleaded one woman. "They cannot make laws or elect law-makers to obviate or suppress the great evil."

But the spectacle of women marching in the streets produced strong criticism from those who opposed a public role for women. Many newspaper commentaries shared the perspective of the *St. Louis Dispatch*, which declared that "when the wives, mothers, sisters and virgins of the land break down the barriers of that precious isolation public opinion has provided for their protection, and spring into the arena, flushed and disheveled, unsexed, and already tainted . . . when [woman] goes among men to preach, and pray, and wrestle with them in prayer . . . she will need, because of her undoing, more prayers to make her pure again than would have saved all the rumsellers between New York and San Francisco."

Some churches, normally supportive of temperance initiatives, balked at women's militance. Friends of temperance and women's rights who put their faith in legal action also wavered in their support of the Crusades. The temperance lodges and the Prohibition party, despite their admiration for the Crusaders, nevertheless viewed direct action as a return to the fruitless strategy of moral suasion and therefore a distraction from the important task of passing prohibition laws. Woman suffragists were also mixed in their reaction to the Crusades. Elizabeth Cady Stanton, for one, considered direct action to be a dubious exercise in "mob law." With others, she counseled aggrieved women to work for the vote to attain public influence. Although suffrage advocates could be found in Crusader ranks, the bulk of the women involved in the anti-saloon campaigns had not yet shown much interest in suffrage—they were focused instead on saving their families. Direct action had inspired these women, but it also tangled up the movement's relationship with potential allies.

Before a year had passed, the forces of the law that had earlier failed women brought a halt to the Crusades. Uncomfortable with encounters in the streets and on the sawdust-covered floors of barrooms, male supporters of the Women's Crusade urged a shift to legal channels of reform. The passage of new prohibition or tighter license regulations in many towns, along with the promise to enforce existing ordinances, helped accomplish this transformation. These laws, along with the impact of the economic depression of 1873 and internal consolidation in the brewing and distilling industries, temporarily reduced the number of retail liquor outlets. In places where the Crusade had struggled or met rowdy opposition, municipal governments shut down street demonstrations by selectively enforcing nuisance laws against Crusaders. Finally, the enthusiasm and spontaneity of the Women's Crusade provided the opportunity for the formation of a centralized, organized women's temperance body. It would reorient the female struggle against alcohol to accommodate the legal, political, and hierarchical structure of the Gilded Age. That organization, formed in November 1874, was the Woman's Christian Temperance Union.

4

Prohibition in the Gilded Age

DURING THE WINTER of 1873–1874, desperate women had taken to the streets to close down the liquor traffic in their communities. The system of law and politics had denied them a formal workable means through which to defend their loved ones from the perils of intemperance. Women's marginalized political status made direct action a solemn necessity. By contrast, the Woman's Christian Temperance Union, which flourished after 1874, intended to open the political system to women's influence and thereby bring temperance reform and women's activism into the political mainstream.

In one sense the WCTU's political orientation matched the outlook of the Gilded Age. The period between the end of Reconstruction and the turbulent 1890s is notable as the golden age of political participation in the United States. Voter turnout was remarkably high—up to 80 percent of eligible voters—and political affairs generated popular enthusiasm on a scale that would baffle modern observers. In a culture in which political activity frequently reflected one's basic identity, WCTU women managed to carve out a respected position for themselves in public life. On the other hand, by advocating prohibition, the WCTU undermined a central tenet of the Gilded Age political system—consistent loyalty to one of the two major parties. As WCTU activists worked to build a political movement dedicated to prohibition, Republican and Democratic officials, fearing damaging internal splits over the restriction of alcohol, struggled to confine the issue to local communities and avoid official party positions on prohibition in state and national campaigns. The resulting strain between prohibition enthusiasts and party professionals became a major feature of local and state politics in the 1880s, as ethnic conflict over liquor restriction overwhelmed party discipline in the Midwest. Although it failed in its most ambitious attempts at reform, the WCTU helped bring prohibition back into American politics and disrupt the Gilded Age political system.

On its founding the WCTU shared the religious imagery and emphasis on moral suasion that characterized the Women's Crusade. But, quite unlike the grass-roots Crusade, the new organization developed out of more formal ties to evangelical Protestantism. It quickly moved away from the direct-action confrontations made famous by the marching women. Women active in the Protestant Sunday-school and home-mission movements arranged the Cleveland meeting that formed the WCTU; Annie Wittenmyer, editor of a Methodist newspaper and architect of the Methodist Home Missionary Society, was named the first president. Wittenmyer and her allies were proponents of gospel temperance, a strategy aimed at saving drunkards and rehabilitating liquor sellers through mass meetings, prayer, and publicity. These techniques had been used by the Crusaders as well, but often in combination with street demonstrations and barroom showdowns, actions the WCTU rejected. In keeping with the interests of many WCTU organizers in childhood education, the Union also advocated temperance instruction for children in Sunday schools and in public schools. Initially the WCTU seemed content to

operate according to the accepted boundaries of female phil-
anthropic concern.

Hidden inside the conventional framework of the WCTU,
however, were innovative policies that challenged the legal
subordination of American women, helped revive prohibition
as a political force, and built the WCTU into one of the
largest, most influential reform associations of the late nineteenth century (with almost 150,000 dues-paying members in
1890). Unlike most female reform groups, the WCTU barred
men from voting membership, thus ensuring women's control
of its course. Despite the absence of explicit commitments to
political action or mention of woman suffrage in the organizing convention, there were also hints that the WCTU contained the seeds of an active political outlook. WCTU locals
were organized by congressional districts, for instance, and
the organization quickly petitioned Congress to investigate
the liquor industry. More important, Frances Willard, for-
merly dean of Northwestern Ladies College, secretary of the
politically minded Illinois WCTU, and a charismatic, articu-
late advocate of women's advancement, in 1874 was named
corresponding secretary of the national body. Within a year
Willard was pushing the WCTU to develop a broader, clearly
political agenda which would address women's rights as well
as temperance. In 1876, at the urging of its local Unions, the
WCTU endorsed the passage of state prohibition laws and, in
response to Willard's measured prodding, began to debate the
volatile question of woman suffrage. In 1879 Willard edged
out Wittenmyer to assume the presidency of the Union, a position she held, with slight breaks, until her death in 1898.

The dynamism and influence of the WCTU over the next
twenty years was linked to the extraordinary popularity of
Frances Willard as a reform leader and symbol of womanly
virtue. During the 1880s she inspired an organization of

middle-class, mainly conservative women to take bold political action and agitate for a wide variety of reforms. Her impact was such that, years after Willard's death, WCTU locals in small New York towns celebrated her birthday and reverently read from her works. Willard's success in making temperance the centerpiece of a web of women's activism derived from her unusual ability to combine mainstream Protestant sensibilities and conformity to the ideals of Victorian womanhood with a deep personal commitment to woman suffrage, gender reform, and radical political notions. In short, she managed to embody domesticity while working to remove many of the limitations imposed on American women by the culture of domesticity.

Despite a life filled with political maneuvering and platform oratory, a newspaper obituary memorialized Willard as a woman whose considerable "mental faculties were not cultivated at the expense of the gentler side of her nature." Willard's appeal was deepened by a remarkable personal magnetism, described by the historian Ruth Bordin as an "intense, almost sexual attractiveness to members of her own sex" that inspired devoted loyalty from many WCTU women. Even the conservative South, which resisted woman suffrage and other reform innovations, fell under Willard's spell. She made two notable swings through the South—in 1881 and 1883— that built the WCTU into a truly national organization and helped energize Southern temperance efforts.

Willard overcame the hesitancy within the WCTU to embrace woman suffrage by arguing that women's unique interest in religion, home, and family compelled them to take defensive political action against the corrupting influences that assailed those precious institutions. Already a committed suffragist in her personal views, in 1876 she chose a temperance camp meeting in Maine to make a conservative—even reactionary—case for women to demand the vote. Before an audience of evangelical Methodists, Willard declared that "the ballot has been prostituted to undermine the Sabbath, and rob our children of the influence of the Bible in our schools." Women, "truest to God and our country by instinct and education, should have a voice at the polls, where the Sabbath and the Bible are now attacked by the infidel foreign population of our country." This type of bluntly nativist appeal was rare for Willard, but it took the radical edge off her suffrage proposal by framing it in terms of traditional Protestant allegiances.

Later that year she urged the WCTU to endorse what she brilliantly called the "home-protection ballot." Drawing on the concerns that had motivated the Women's Crusade, Willard asked that, instead of relying on men, the "mothers and daughters of America" be allowed to determine whether "the door of the rum shop is opened or shut beside their homes." Willard's formulation presented female suffrage not as a disruptive departure from accepted gender roles but as a means to guarantee the sanctity of the hearthside. In 1881, commitment to the home-protection ballot became official WCTU policy.

As a natural extension of women's domestic concerns and temperance work, the WCTU under Willard embarked on a broad agenda of reforms, incorporated into a strategy that the charismatic president labeled "Do Everything." Jailhouse visits to preach temperance acquainted middle-class WCTU members with the peculiar problems of female inmates. Soon the WCTU became involved in the prison reform movement, asking that female matrons be hired to oversee women prisoners and arguing for the establishment of halfway houses to help rehabilitate released convicts. Sunday school temperance lessons introduced the Union to child protection, which expanded to include concern for child workers, homeless, unsupervised, or abused children, and support for the kindergarten movement. WCTU activists also worked to eliminate the sexual double standard, participated in the "social purity" fight against prostitution, endorsed women's health and legal reforms, and studied leisure alternatives to the working-class saloon. Following Willard, some WCTU women began to conclude that the alcohol problem was bound up in other social debilities: the inadequacy of women's political power, the mistreatment of children and prisoners, poverty, labor's weakness. A few even came to believe, with Willard, that poverty and hopelessness bred alcohol dependency, rather than the reverse.

In some localities the WCTU became an instrument through which women challenged more ironclad social conventions. Such was the case in North Carolina, where WCTU activism between 1881 and 1898 crossed the South's increasingly rigid racial divide. Temperance women organized separate black and white chapters of a common state WCTU, which the historian Glenda Gilmore identifies as "the first postbellum statewide biracial voluntary organization in North Carolina." Although white women were awkward and patronizing in their relationships with black WCTU women, their interracial initiative nevertheless ran against the grain of male-dominated public policy. For black women, involvement in the WCTU promoted racial uplift and established healing ties of gender solidarity and middle-class respectability across the painful barrier of race. Gilmore argues that "African American women used the WCTU to point up black dignity, industriousness, and good citizenship," thereby making a case for full black participation in the public life of North Carolina. In 1889 black WCTU women took a further step away from subordination by seceding from the state WCTU and establishing their own organization, named

WCTU No. 2, which communicated directly with the national Union. The black women "cautiously avoided using the word colored" for their association, "for we believe all men equal." Thus some WCTU branches moved beyond Willard in their radical sentiments.

Willard's reform programs sparked occasional opposition and were largely downplayed in the South, but the political strategies she championed aroused greater controversy. Although the great majority of Northern WCTU members felt ties of loyalty to the Republican party and white Southerners were committed Democrats, Willard worked in the 1880s to forge an alliance with the Prohibition party, the only political organization willing to endorse the WCTU goals of the home-protection ballot and constitutional prohibition. In 1882 Willard tried to unite the WCTU and the Prohibitionists in the renamed Prohibition Home Protection party, but the WCTU national convention stopped shy of outright endorsement of the Prohibition party.

The strongest resistance to Willard's effort to join the WCTU to the Prohibitionists came from J. Ellen Foster, the Union's superintendent of legislation and a dedicated Republican. Foster countered Willard's wooing of the Prohibition party by lobbying the national GOP to win a hearing for WCTU proposals and, on the state level, organizing referendum campaigns to enact constitutional prohibition. Her success in winning Republican support in Iowa for constitutional prohibition in 1882 encouraged Republican loyalists within the WCTU. Nevertheless, Willard successfully aligned the WCTU with the Prohibitionists, prompting Foster to lead a disgruntled splinter group—mainly from Iowa and Pennsylvania—out of the Union in 1889 to form a rival Non-Partisan Woman's Christian Temperance Union. Reflecting the political status of American women, the WCTU had cast its lot with those on the margins of the political power structure.

Willard meanwhile sought to stitch together a grand alliance of radicals and the politically dispossessed. The cooperation of the WCTU with Prohibitionists introduced additional reform planks into the Prohibition party platform, most notably an endorsement of woman suffrage. Willard also engineered an informal alliance with the Knights of Labor in 1886, which in turn agreed to support woman suffrage and cooperated on several legislative ventures. By the late 1880s, influenced by Edward Bellamy's utopian novel *Looking Backward*, Willard had become a Christian Socialist, adding pacifism and international arbitration to her reform portfolio. Restiveness within the national Union over wide-ranging WCTU commitments to radical-sounding principles grew stronger. Many local Unions simply ignored Willard's larger programs to concentrate on temperance reform at home. Between 1889 and 1892, Willard dodged the criticism and labored to craft a fusion movement between the WCTU, the Prohibition party, and the Populists, the radical voice of aggrieved farmers. But the proposed union failed to materialize when the Prohibition party refused to compromise its positions to suit the Populists.

The 1890s, in the words of Jack Blocker, marked a "retreat from reform" for the temperance movement as the "Do Everything" viewpoint withered away. By the time of Willard's death, the WCTU had moved back to a single-minded focus on temperance. During the same decade the Prohibition party split over the question of "broad-gauged" reform, one faction holding out for commitment to an extensive reform agenda but the majority in the party returning to an exclusive emphasis on prohibition. This dispute eroded the small influ-

ence the party enjoyed in the 1880s and consigned the Prohibition party to political insignificance.

For two decades Willard's premise that true temperance reform required attention to a host of interrelated social ills had
directed organized prohibition work. That outlook, however,
was more in keeping with the "alternative America" envisioned by alienated social critics like Bellamy and embattled
producer groups such as the Knights of Labor and the Populists than with the cautious mainstream of the late nineteenth
century. The strength and resiliency of the two-party system
overwhelmed the enthusiasm of the WCTU–Prohibition
party alliance. Prohibition in the early twentieth century
would have greater success by emphasizing the middle-class
roots of the temperance outlook, stripping away divisive companion issues, and bypassing third-party crusades in favor of
influencing elected officials and the major parties. The Anti-
Saloon League became the chief proponent of this approach,
though the WCTU, after the Willard era, provided effective
assistance by conforming to political orthodoxy. For example,
by 1898 the North Carolina WCTU had embraced the Democratic party platform of white supremacy and halted its interracial initiatives. The WCTU ironically reached its objective
of national prohibition by turning its back on the strategy of
its beloved leader.

In the heart of the Gilded Age, however, Willard and the
WCTU reignited women's political activism and revived temperance reform as a political issue that could not be dismissed.
In her study of political values and action in New York State,
for example, the historian Paula Baker found that in the late
nineteenth century, "temperance became the cause that most
visibly absorbed rural women in public life." WCTU women
and their allies in the Grange, the country's premier rural association, lobbied, passed out ballots, and served food during

village license elections. They petitioned state government to enact the WCTU "scientific temperance education" proposal; after passage in 1884, one local sent representatives to the schoolhouse to ensure that the proper lessons were imparted. (By 1900 nearly every state had enacted measures requiring public schools to teach children that alcohol was a poison, using textbooks screened by the WCTU.) They lobbied state representatives to pass restrictive liquor laws and complained bitterly when the governor vetoed one such bill. This political toughness was also apparent at the local level; when "whiskey-ites" hurled a dead skunk into a room in which women were preparing food during an 1887 license election, the women, rather than retreating, scooped up no-license ballots, marched to the polls, and, enduring the taunts and spittle of male "row-dies," successfully urged voters to eradicate the local bars.

Across the country in the 1880s, contests turning on the prohibition of liquor sales became a mainstay of village, town, and county politics and began to appear at the state level as well. The home-protection ballot was still rarely available— by 1890 women could vote on school issues in seventeen states, and Kansas had extended municipal suffrage to women, but only Wyoming provided full woman suffrage. When Carry Nation shocked public opinion by destroying several illegal Kansas saloons between 1900 and 1901, she justified her actions with a complaint that recalled the saloon attacks of the 1850s and the desperation that preceded the Women's Crusade. "You refused me the vote," she told the Kansas legislature, "and I had to use a rock." But Carry Nation was an anomaly at the end of the nineteenth century. Rather than turning away from the system of law and politics, American women learned from the WCTU to force parties and government to confront the liquor issue. Aided by women's activism, a new politics of morality and cultural conflict overwhelmed the resistance of party professionals in some states and returned prohibition to the public agenda of the late nineteenth century.

The major parties maintained the political equilibrium of the Gilded Age by emphasizing party identification and loyalty. Divisive questions that might fracture party unity were contained at the local level; in national campaigns, the Democrats and Republicans focused on abstruse issues such as currency inflation and the tariff in order to highlight their distinctive positions and minimize disunity. For individual Republicans or Democrats, party identification did not depend on issues so much as on cultural traditions, family ties, and custom. An Ohio Republican remembered that in the 1870s and 1880s, membership in the GOP "was not a matter of intellectual choice, it was a process of biological selection." The party "was merely a synonym for patriotism, another name for the nation." But in the 1880s, after the Women's Crusade and during the WCTU's most active period, the Democratic adherence to "personal liberty" and the Republican celebration of progress hardened into an intense struggle in local communities, especially in the Midwest and Northeast, to determine standards of private behavior and public control. Angry fights over the licensing of saloons, public school policies, public support for parochial schools, and Sunday amusements bubbled up from small towns, cities, and counties to disturb political harmony, particularly among Republicans, at the state level.

Historians have discerned ethnic and cultural dimensions to these struggles. Christians coming from evangelical or pietistic confessional traditions that laid stress on individual conduct—Methodists, Congregationalists, Presbyterians, most Baptists, Scandinavian Lutherans, and most smaller Protestant denominations—tended to back prohibition and oppose tax support for Catholic schools and the relaxed Continental Sunday. Those whose faith stressed church traditions and liturgical richness—primarily Catholics, German Lutherans, and Episcopalians—often interpreted Sunday blue laws and liquor regulations as outrageous restrictions on personal freedom and cultural traditions. Of course, most Irish, German, and central European immigrants were liturgicals, and many natives belonged to pietist faiths, adding an explosive ethnic cast to cultural politics. As cultural issues began to overtake the safer party topics of the Gilded Age, existing political coalitions were disrupted, particularly in the Midwest where German Lutherans were an important element of GOP majorities. Prohibition was the most common and destabilizing of these "ethnocultural" issues.

Natives and immigrants reacted strongly to prohibition because the issue of liquor regulation politicized highly sensitive attitudes about the integrity of the family and the stability of the social order. Many native Protestant households felt themselves under assault from a reckless saloon trade that separated husbands from wives and parents from children, and refused to reform itself. In defense of their families, they marshaled the weapons of democracy—political parties, the public schools, and ultimately the power of the state—to defend community standards and suppress the noxious traffic in intoxicants. European immigrant households—Catholic and Lutheran Germans, Bohemians, and Irish, among others—defined the threat to families and the civic order in a radically different way. Whereas native Protestants turned to the law, common schools, and other public institutions to safeguard their cultural values, the historian Jon Gjerde argues that German immigrants in the rural Midwest believed that those institutions undermined the authority of parents over their children, weakened cultural bonds, and threatened to drive a

wedge of governmental interference through the daily interaction of inoffensive households. Whereas WCTU women
saw themselves as engaged in "home protection," German
newspapermen in Iowa renounced "temperance witches" and
woman suffrage advocates who by their brazen entry into
public affairs had emasculated their husbands and disgraced
their families.

At bottom, for many immigrants, prohibition revealed a
strain of American fanaticism that dismissed the moderating
influences of tradition, family, and individual self-control and
insisted on the humiliating restrictions of legal compulsion.
Such feelings prompted another Iowa German in 1887 to
complain that "a few *fanatics* who indicate that they themselves haven't the moral backbone to look at a glass of beer, or
pass a saloon without getting drunk, come along and tell me
that I am incapable of behaving myself or keeping sober, and
so they propose to take care of me by law." Although both
Yankees and immigrants acted to shield their families from
disorderly influences and to promote civic harmony, their fun-
damentally different conceptions of those ideals provoked
boisterous conflict.

Republican politicians were well aware of the volatility of
prohibition and worked to avoid it as a party question. During
the 1880s both public officials and the beleaguered liquor industry supported more expensive annual saloon licenses—
usually from $500 to $1,000—as an alternative to prohibition.
High license fees would presumably restrict the trade to a
smaller number of better-class establishments and reduce the
incidence of drunkenness, violence, prostitution, and Sunday-
closing violations that had aroused public protest. Beginning
in Kansas in 1879, however, dedicated bands of temperance
Republicans shrugged off high license and undertook grass-
roots campaigns to force prohibition on their party. Their

weapons were the constitutional referendum and the threat to defect to the Prohibition party should the GOP fail to embrace prohibition. In Kansas the referendum campaign was led by Republican governor and ardent temperance backer John St. John, the Kansas State Temperance Union, and the WCTU. Rallying around the KSTU admonition to "vote as you pray," Kansans in 1880 approved a constitutional amendment banning "the manufacture and sale of intoxicating liquors." In Iowa, one of the strongest Republican states in the nation, hesitant party officials were swept aside in 1882 as a collection of rank-and-file pietists successfully engineered the adoption of a similar amendment. The elated victors declared that in Iowa, "Republicanism" now meant "a school house on every hill, and no saloon in the valley."

Between 1883 and 1890, sixteen more states—Ohio, Maine, Rhode Island, Michigan, Oregon, Tennessee, Texas, West Virginia, Connecticut, Massachusetts, New Hampshire, North Dakota, South Dakota, Pennsylvania, Washington, and Nebraska—voted on prohibition amendments. Maine reaffirmed its prohibition stance, Rhode Island adopted prohibition but quickly repealed it, and the Dakotas joined Kansas and Iowa as new prohibition states. Even where constitutional prohibition was defeated, local option laws that allowed counties or municipalities to ban liquor sales often appeared, and Republican officeholders in the North were forced by prohibitionist sentiment to strengthen Sunday-closing laws.

The national Republican party felt the sting of the prohibition question in the 1884 presidential election. Dry Republicans were unhappy with the party's candidate, James G. Blaine, a reputed spoilsman who refused to address the liquor question. In an extremely close loss to Democrat Grover Cleveland, Blaine and the Republicans were undercut by both sides of the liquor issue. In New York, Republican defections to the Prohibition party cost Blaine the state by about a thousand votes, which denied him the presidency. On the other hand, while campaigning in the Empire State the inattentive Blaine failed to hear a Protestant minister speaking on his behalf excoriate the Democrats as the party of "Rum, Romanism, and Rebellion." When the unknowing candidate let the slanderous remark stand, any immigrant, Catholic, or anti-prohibitionist support he may have used to counteract the loss of prohibitionist Republican votes disappeared as well.

After its 1884 defeat, the GOP employed the WCTU's Ellen Foster to urge dry Republican women to avoid the lures of the prohibitionists and use their influence to buttress Republicanism. Republicans also inserted a soothing statement into their 1888 platform, affirming sympathy for "all wise and well-directed efforts for the production of temperance." Still, Republican leaders, anxious not to "alienate anybody," kept prohibition out of party newspapers and avoided firm positions on the issue.

The political wisdom of this course was demonstrated in 1889 and 1890, when the Midwestern GOP was stunned by a series of shocking defeats related to ethnic and cultural issues. The disruptive effects of prohibition on Republican unity had been displayed in Kansas in 1882, when anti-prohibition Republicans had united with Democrats to deny Governor St. John a third term. (St. John went on to become the Prohibition party presidential nominee in 1884.) Iowans, whom Republican Jonathan Dolliver confidently predicted in 1883 would "go Democratic when hell goes Methodist," elected Democrat Horace Boies governor in 1889. Boies had deserted the GOP because of the prohibition amendment, accompanied by large numbers of alienated German Republicans who had their revenge at the polls. Disaster also befell Ohio Republican governor Joseph Foraker, whose enforcement of Sunday closing led to his defeat the same year. According to a German newspaper from Cincinnati, Germans "knocked the Republican party into smithereens" because of their unhappiness with Ohio's high license law and Sunday-closing policy.

Ill-considered laws that required English-language instruction for all schools, both public and private, prompted further German defections and Democratic victories in Illinois and Wisconsin in 1890. Both in Congress and in statehouses across the country that year, Republicans suffered defeats in the backlash against the pietist-prohibition agitation of the 1880s. German voters were not coaxed back to the Republican fold until the mid-1890s. After that debacle the Republican party, though still harboring the great majority of temperance-minded voters, approached liquor regulation with extreme caution. Public sentiment would be carefully measured before commitments were proffered.

In the South, where the appearance of local-option laws during the 1880s signaled the renewal of temperance sentiment, the Democratic party also was divided on whether to extend official support to dry initiatives. An 1881 popular referendum to adopt prohibition in North Carolina, for example, failed badly after many Democratic leaders, fearing that state Republicans would gain political advantages should prohibition become law, turned against the measure just before the election. A Democratic politician in Tennessee admitted that many loyal Democrats were to be found in the cold-water army, but he warned that "the Republican, the ambitious place hunter, the woman's rights shrieker, the fanatic, and the independent are also there." Throughout the region, Democratic strategists argued that introducing temperance into partisan debates could strengthen the Republicans and promote the formation of Prohibition party organizations in the South, thereby disrupting the political balance of power and threatening to overturn Democratic rule. Political stability required that liquor regulation operate outside the boundaries of standard partisan competition. For all its energy and achievements, organized temperance reform was still regarded with alarm by the political system.

Oddly enough, after the wave of effort and disappointment that marked the 1880s, prohibition was on the threshold of its greatest political achievements. Critical to this shift was the breakdown of the Gilded Age political system of bland issues, predictable voter turnout, and unwavering partisan loyalty under the hammer blows of economic crisis and political challenge. The massive depression of 1893 forced hundreds of banks and thousands of businesses to close, compelled those that remained active to slash wages, and threw up to three million workers out of jobs. In Chicago, where the magnificent Columbian Exposition celebrated human progress in the arts and sciences, city officials opened public buildings at night to provide sleeping space for some of the city's homeless multitudes. Across the nation, clusters of unemployed men gathered near railroad tracks, and newspapers noted a sharp rise in the "tramp problem." The depression also changed American politics. President Grover Cleveland, a traditional Democrat who believed that "while the people should patriotically and cheerfully support their government, its functions do not include the support of the people," became a subject of contempt and ridicule for his attachment to the gold standard and his refusal to provide government relief to those who clamored for it.

Sensing weakness in the Democrats, the Republican party attacked Democratic responses to the depression, promoted itself as the party of prosperity, and actively sought to win over disaffected Democrats. For their part, Democrats jettisoned Cleveland in 1896 and nominated William Jennings Bryan,

who called for currency inflation and more extensive government action to support farmers and workers. The 1896 presidential election between Bryan and William McKinley, the
Republican candidate, set into motion a partisan realignment
that ended the Gilded Age political system. Many Eastern,
urban, and conservative Democrats looked askance at Bryan's
reform proposals and his agrarian rhetoric; some of them
began to vote Republican. The Populist movement also helped
dislodge many Americans from their steadfast attachment to
the major parties. Buried in debt, feeling beset by monopolies,
and angry that their interests were ignored, Western and
Southern farmers concluded that "the controlling influences
dominating the old political parties have allowed the existing
dreadful conditions to develop without serious effort to restrain or prevent them." The farmers joined a coalition of reformers in launching the People's party, which between 1892
and 1896 vigorously challenged political orthodoxy. Even
though the Populist revolt was short-lived, it shook up party
politics and awakened many Americans to the possibilities of
forceful government action to promote the public welfare.
After 1896 American voters were less mindful of party loyalties, more likely to sit out elections, and more open to the appeal of particular issues and their disciplined advocates.

   Although Frances Willard's hope for a Populist–Prohibition party alliance dissolved and the politics of depression focused on economic issues rather than intemperance, the
reshuffling of politics in the 1890s enabled a new approach to
temperance reform to take hold after the turn of the century.
Avoiding the factional squabbles of party politics, Progressive
Era reformers, health professionals, and social investigators
offered a fresh nonpartisan indictment of saloons and the alcoholic drink trades. To these critics, the traffic in intoxicants
endangered the prosperous development of a modern urban,

industrial society. Temperance reform had never managed to exist comfortably within the structure of late-nineteenth-century party politics. During the Progressive Era, it was the saloon that became marginalized.

5

Alcohol and the Saloon in the Progressive Era

DURING the nineteenth century, temperance reform had reflected the hopeful expectations and anxieties of a rapidly changing society. As the United States became a modern industrialized, urban nation between 1890 and 1920, the prohibition movement revived. Beginning in 1907 a new and stronger wave of state prohibition laws rolled across the country and culminated in the passage and ratification of the 18th Amendment to the Constitution, which barred the production, transfer, and sale of alcoholic beverages throughout the United States after midnight, January 16, 1920.

Despite the early-nineteenth-century roots of temperance reform, the drive toward prohibition in this period mirrored the dominant themes of modernizing America—bureaucracy, expertise, and professionalization. A new generation of temperance workers, led by the Anti-Saloon League of America, opportunistically employed the techniques of the emerging organizational society to overcome the partisan political tangles that had obstructed prohibition initiatives in the past. The appeal of these new methods of temperance reform was grounded in mounting evidence of the social dangers posed by the organized liquor traffic and its most common neighborhood manifestation, the saloon. The impersonal forces of industrialization, urbanization, and immigration that rearranged the liquor industry in the Progressive Era also helped transform prohibitionist sentiment into a modern social movement.

Between 1890 and 1920 the recognizable features of modern America took shape. The transformation from a society of rural villages and small towns sustained by agriculture and mercantile enterprise into a largely urban, highly industrialized nation, which had unfolded over the course of the nineteenth century, accelerated sharply. In 1890 officials of the Census Bureau declared the American frontier closed—the nation had been settled from coast to coast. By 1920 most Americans resided in communities that the Census Bureau defined as urban (2,500 or more people). During the same period the number of large American cities more than doubled, increasing from 28 cities of over 100,000 inhabitants in 1890 to 68 urban centers of that size in 1920. More striking than these general patterns were the physical manifestations of modernity: colossal cities exhibiting the new urban architecture of skyscrapers, public parks, and "streetcar suburbs"; the plants and office complexes of large corporations created by the business consolidations of the 1890s; even the telephones and interurban railways that linked smaller cities into a dense metropolitan network. To a considerable degree, as the historian Samuel Hays has argued, Americans at the turn of the century lived in an "organizational society" in which economic, professional, or occupational ties intruded upon the traditional bonds of family, religion, or community.

One of the products of modernizing America was a "new middle class" that, in a flurry of reform activity known as progressivism, sought to solve social and political problems through bureaucratic means. Progressive reformers urged university-trained lawyers, social workers, public health experts, and city planners to work as representatives of the public interest in a crusade to bring order and justice to a society shaken by several decades of chaotic, unregulated expansion. During the 1890s the passage into modernity had been accompanied by economic depression, labor strife, bewilderment and anger on the part of farmers, and a wave of racial violence and repression in the South. Industrial and urban growth was sustained by an unprecedented influx of immigrants from unfamiliar regions of eastern and southern Europe. Native-born Americans eyed the newcomers with mingled compassion and alarm—compassion for the poverty, overcrowding, and dangerous working conditions that afflicted immigrants; alarm at the alien folkways that many feared would undermine American customs. While admiring the efficiency of modern corporations, progressives worried about the power of corporate wealth and expressed shock at the gulf separating the rich from the majority of their fellow citizens. Progressive reformers attempted to use the power of government to correct these inequities and construct an urban, industrial society that was safe, efficient, and humane.

Despite the dominant industrial mind-set of the Progressive Era, powerful traditional beliefs and outright resistance to the demands of the industrial ethos persisted into the twentieth century. Few Americans, even among the modernizers of the new middle class, had abandoned older values in favor of a resolute march into the future. The precise methods of social scientific inquiry employed by progressive social workers, economists, and factory inspectors were often inspired by a Christian commitment to reform or, as in the case of the settlement-house pioneer Jane Addams, a "passion of conciliation" grounded in the experiences of a small-town childhood.

Just as in the mid-nineteenth century, reform activism in the
Progressive Era reflected a middle-class dedication to order,
progress, and community cohesion.

Traditional patterns of behavior in defiance of the industrial system of labor were more pronounced among immigrants and the native-born working class. Workers intent on
preserving their autonomy resisted both factory discipline and
attempts on the part of employers and reformers alike to regulate their leisure time. Pre-industrial habits of life and labor
were reinforced by the "new immigration." Beginning in the
1880s and cresting between 1900 and 1910, millions of Italians,
Slavs, Greeks, and Russian Jews joined the older immigrant
streams from Ireland, Germany, and Scandinavia to populate
American cities and fill the industrial labor force. By 1910 immigrants and their children made up more than 70 percent of
the population of Boston, Buffalo, Chicago, Cleveland, De-
troit, Milwaukee, and New York. As the historian Herbert
Gutman has observed, massive immigration along with internal migration produced a continuous introduction "of peas-
ants, farmers, skilled artisans, and casual day laborers who
brought into industrial society ways of work and other habits
and values not associated with industrial necessities" or the behavioral codes favored by middle-class Americans. Together,
as the historian Roy Rosenzweig has demonstrated, immigrants and the native-born working class forged a vibrant "alternative culture" of work and leisure in which the saloon and
the enjoyment of strong drink figured prominently as symbols
of community and autonomy.

As Americans strained to adjust to their new nation, alcohol again became a forceful public issue. As in the early nineteenth century, temperance reform at the turn of the century
was the product of new economic and social circumstances, an
upsurge of optimistic reform sentiment and organized reli-

gious activism, and a cultural struggle to define behavioral norms for American society. Yet the renewed assault on drinking also reflected the emergence of the new bureaucratized, urban mass society. Just as in other reform endeavors in the Progressive Era, anti-liquor advocates drew on the authority of experts and the methods of social investigation to bring civilized order out of what appeared to be the chaos of modern life.

Doctors and social scientists reassessed the impact of strong drink on the physical and economic well-being of individuals and families, on safety and efficiency in the workplace, and on the public order. Studies of the children of alcoholic parents demonstrated the devastating effects of excessive drinking into the next generation. Investigations of the impact of alcohol on the central nervous system offered evidence of the health risks associated with even moderate drinking. In 1915 whiskey and brandy, once popular as medicinal beverages, were dropped from the list of medically approved drugs. Shortly before the triumph of national prohibition, the American Medical Association condemned "the use of alcohol as a beverage." The conclusions of the medical profession were buttressed by actuarial studies conducted by the insurance industry, which charted significantly higher mortality rates for drinkers over abstainers.

Progressive Era experts were also attentive to the social and economic costs of drinking. The Committee of Fifty, a prominent group of professional men investigating the "liquor problem," in 1899 published nearly seventy pages of tables detailing the relationship of drinking to poverty, pauperism, neglect of children, and crime. Others probed the influence of drinking on business enterprise. The increased mechanization of industry, the appearance of workers' compensation and employers' liability laws, and heightened interest in industrial

efficiency during the Progressive Era all influenced a movement to improve workplace safety and employee perfor-
mance. The persistent working-class custom of drinking on
the job challenged efficiency and safety experts. One Chicago
saloon in 1900 "sold ninety gallons [of beer] every noon to men
in a factory and to a railroad gang." The presence of alcohol in
the long struggle between employers and workers for control
of the shop floor gave a special intensity to progressive efforts
to eliminate liquor from the workplace. Although middle-
class professionals differed on the wisdom of prohibition, their
commitment to discipline, order, and progress made them
critics of working-class culture's attachment to strong drink.

In the context of industrialization and urban ills, the disorderly and dangerous consequences of an unregulated culture
of male drinking once more began to alarm middle-class
Americans, especially as it came to be associated with the Old
World customs of immigrants, expressions of working-class
cultural independence, and the spread of vice. One Chicago
clergyman feared "a foreign invasion" of undemocratic values
from the spread of immigrant drinking culture. The progressive belief in the powerful influence of the environment on
children raised further concern. It was commonplace in turn-
of-the-century American cities for children to collect pails at
factory gates, fill them with beer at saloons, and bring them
to lunching workmen, a practice known as "rushing the
growler." Such early and continued exposure to the culture of
drinking, to say nothing of the easy access to intoxicating
drinks, disturbed the "child savers" of the Progressive Era, especially settlement residents such as Jane Addams and a growing corps of social workers who were determined to improve
conditions in urban neighborhoods. Investigations into the
underworld of prostitution, carried out by vice commissions

in more than a hundred American cities between 1902 and 1916, implicated the liquor trade in the troubling expansion of the "social evil." "As a contributory influence to immorality and the business of prostitution there is no interest so danger-ous and so powerful" as the saloon, judged the influential Chicago Vice Commission in a representative conclusion. Charges that brewers and distillers destroyed lives, corrupted minors, and exercised undue political influence intensified as the Progressive Era unfolded. At the center of each of these concerns was the immigrant, working-class saloon, described by one prohibitionist as "the acme of evil, the climax of iniq-uity, the mother of abominations, and the sum of villainies."

Saloons attracted such extravagant denunciation because they were the physical and symbolic centerpiece of a revived culture of drinking. Together, tradition and the dynamics of modernity again altered American drinking patterns in sig-nificant new ways. After decades of relative stability, alcohol consumption began to rise sharply after 1900. Americans of drinking age (fifteen years and older) drank an average of 2.1 gallons of pure alcohol in 1900; by 1910 their alcohol intake had increased to 2.6 gallons, the highest figure since 1840. But the manner and the context of drinking in 1900 was quite dis-tinctive from that of 1840. The culture of American drinking in the early nineteenth century had centered on whiskey; the late nineteenth century inaugurated the age of beer. The in-crease in beer consumption during that period was dramatic. In the early 1880s Americans drank about a half-million gal-lons of beer. By the early 1890s that figure had doubled to a million gallons and by 1913 had doubled again to two million gallons. More significant, beer displaced distilled liquor as the primary source of alcohol consumed in America. At the be-ginning of the 1870s distilled liquor had accounted for 80 percent of the alcohol consumed in the United States. By 1915, despite a revival of spirits-drinking after 1900, 60 percent of the alcohol consumed by Americans came from beer.

Three of the central forces that shaped modern America— immigration, industrialization, and urbanization—by 1900 helped turn the United States into a beer-drinking society. The impact of immigration on the American culture of drinking was substantial. German immigrants had introduced lager beer to the United States in the mid-nineteenth century. Germans viewed beer as a food, "liquid bread," which was a necessary accompaniment of family life and community recreation and a healthy alternative to distilled liquor. When assailed by temperance activists, some brewers referred to their product, with its comparatively low alcohol content of about 5 percent, as the ideal "temperance beverage." Reinforced by further waves of immigration from central Europe and the enthusiasm of its advocates, the German fondness for beer spread more generally through American culture by the early twentieth century. Only in the rural South, the region least affected by immigration, did the whiskey habit prevail against the new thirst for beer.

Technological improvements in the brewing industry, the dynamics of business consolidation and competition in the late nineteenth century, and the concentration of population into cities were also critical factors in the rise of beer as the alcoholic drink of choice. Until the 1880s beer was much harder to market than distilled liquor. Unlike whiskey, which was bottled in small containers and could be easily stored for long periods, beer was bulky and extremely perishable. Lager beer, the lighter, pleasant-tasting brew that Americans preferred, required storage at cool temperatures to remain fresh. Consequently brewers produced small batches of their product for immediate local consumption. Large numbers of small or moderate-sized breweries (there were nearly 3,700 firms producing beer in 1867) competed with one another for these small markets.

In the 1880s brewing began to become a big business. The development of mechanical refrigeration, refinements in the brewing process that allowed for greater volume of production, a better integrated transportation network, and rapid urban population growth together matched an expanded demand for beer with a larger and more reliable supply. Midwestern brewers such as Pabst, Schlitz, Blatz, Lemp, and Moerlein began to market their beer nationally, setting off vigorous competition with local brewers. As production and transportation techniques improved, the industry began to consolidate. The number of breweries dropped to 1,500 in 1899 and then to 1,250 in 1914. By then half the beer produced in the United States was brewed by the top 100 firms.

As the brewing industry modernized, however, it developed closer ties to the traditional symbol of intemperance, the urban saloon. The technological innovations that made it easier to ship and store beer for retail sale had not yet made home consumption feasible. Although techniques for bottling beer had been developed by the 1890s, the costs involved in shipping bottled beer and retrieving empty bottles for reuse limited the appeal of the new method. As late as 1915 only 15 percent of the country's beer was bottled. And until the widespread availability of home refrigeration in the 1920s, few Americans could store beer at home. Throughout the Progressive Era, the most direct and economical means to slake the national thirst for beer was in the form of draft beer sold in saloons, an unpasteurized product that had to be consumed quickly. Saloons stored beer in large thirty-one- to fifty-five-

gallon barrels and served large numbers of customers efficiently, thereby combining high volume with maximum
freshness. Thus did the age of beer fortify saloon culture.

Fierce competition in the brewing trade in the 1880s led the
brewers into an even closer relationship with saloons. Most saloonkeepers ran small establishments which could afford to
keep only one or two barrels in stock, so they usually sold a
single brand of beer. In urban markets, where several brewers
vied for the saloon trade, vigorous competition led beer sales-
men to offer free merchandise such as calendars, advertising
displays, glassware, and large prints (including the famous
Anheuser-Busch depiction of "Custer's Last Fight") as well as
discounts and even secret rebates on the beer itself if saloonkeepers would buy their product exclusively. This period of
cutthroat competition, similar to that practiced in other industries at the time, caused a sharp drop in beer prices. In
Chicago, a major beer market, the price of a barrel of beer
plunged from eight dollars to four dollars.

In order to restore prices and to cut the power of independent saloonkeepers, brewers in the last two decades of the
nineteenth century took control of the saloons themselves by
introducing the English tied-house system to the United
States. In return for a fixed monthly payment and a pledge to
sell only a specified brand of beer, brewers would set saloonkeepers up in business. Brewers provided the bar, mirror, taps,
and other fixtures, paid saloon licenses, leased the property,
and sometimes even built the saloons on land they had purchased. By 1916, according to an official investigation in
Chicago, about 70 percent of the city's 7,094 licensed saloons
were "more or less under the control of the breweries." Brewers purchased the liquor licenses for 76 percent of the saloons
in Paterson, New Jersey, in 1908 and more than 80 percent of

those in New York City. All of the 200 saloons in Los Angeles reputedly were owned by breweries. In some cities, such as Boston, wholesale liquor dealers operated saloons through similar methods.

The tied-house system gave brewers a measure of security in the notoriously precarious saloon business. Saloon failures and turnover in ownership were common, but if a saloon-keeper in a tied house sold too little beer and fell behind in his monthly payments, he simply was removed by the brewing firm and a new proprietor brought in to replace him. In addition, the tied-house arrangement often obligated saloonkeepers to pay whatever price the brewer demanded for their beer supply. Saloon operators who wished to offer their customers spirits as well as beer purchased the liquor without the help of the sponsoring brewer. Forced to rely on saloons for the retail sale of beer, brewers nevertheless were determined to reduce the risks to themselves of engaging in that volatile trade.

Saloonkeepers agreed to the tied-house system for different reasons. Some needed help in paying rising saloon license fees. The high-license movement of the 1880s tried to drive marginal and criminal saloons out of business by raising the cost of saloon licenses to $500, $1,000, or even $1,500. An unintended consequence of higher licenses was to push independent saloonkeepers into the arms of the brewers. For others, sponsorship by a brewery offered an otherwise unobtainable opportunity to open a small business with a minimal outlay of capital. As one enthusiastic saloonkeeper put it in 1900, money from brewers made running a saloon "the easiest business in the world to break into." Thousands of working-class Americans with modest savings signed agreements with the brewers and tied on the white apron, many of them hoping eventually to establish themselves as independent proprietors. Compelled by desperation or beckoned by dreams, saloonkeepers throughout the nation entered into formal relationships with the makers of intoxicating drinks.

By 1900 technology, business practices, urban demography, immigration, and other impersonal forces had rearranged the American culture of drinking. But these changes also made possible an intensified moral indictment of the alcoholic beverage industry that significantly strengthened renewed demands for prohibition. The highly visible link between saloons and the manufacturers of strong drink created a perception that the American culture of drinking had spun out of control and once again broke laws, corrupted morals, and threatened the democratic system itself.

First, the adoption of the tied-house system fueled a dangerous overexpansion of the saloon trade. The brewing industry was sufficiently centralized to force many saloonkeepers into the system, but it remained too fragmented to limit the number of such arrangements. As a result, the number of saloons rapidly multiplied. The historian Norman Clark estimates that there were about 150,000 saloons nationwide in 1880 and nearly 300,000 by 1900, the great majority of them concentrated in the urban Northeast and Midwest. Chicago alone had more saloons than the fifteen Southern states combined. Too many saloons, a high level of indebtedness on the part of saloonkeepers, and requirements from the brewery to keep up sales produced a wickedly competitive atmosphere that sometimes transformed the genial neighborhood bartender into a coldhearted profit maximizer. A veteran independent saloonkeeper complained that "a man that has a license controlled by a brewer doesn't care a continental; he runs it to make money." Such observations lent an aura of authenticity to prohibitionist charges that saloonkeepers encouraged cautious patrons to drink to excess, continued to serve problem drinkers past the point of drunkenness, and used tricks to turn boys into adult drinkers.

In a desperate bid to attract customers or supplement insufficient income, some marginal operators turned to illegal methods. They remained open beyond the legal closing time, sold to minors, and watered their drinks. Some saloons approved gambling on the premises; they presented tawdry cabaret acts or allowed prostitutes to solicit men at the bar. A handful even permitted pickpockets to circulate among their customers. Although very few saloons intentionally harbored criminals, a small but noticeable minority of shady places brought suspicion on the entire trade. An experienced representative of the Conrad Seipp Brewing Company estimated that 10 percent of the saloons in Chicago—that is, between seven hundred and eight hundred businesses—were "objectionable." The journalist Jacob Riis reported in 1890 that in New York City "the law prohibiting the selling of beer to minors is about as much respected in the tenement-house districts as the ordinance against swearing." Such examples provided the evidence that helped sustain impressions among the temperance-minded of widespread saloon criminality. "The saloon has the distinction of standing first in this country in the production of crimes and criminals," insisted the sociologist John M. Barker in his 1905 book *The Saloon Problem and Social Reform*. Battered by negative publicity, a trade journal for saloonkeepers (tellingly named *The Champion of Fair Play*) offered weak rebuttals bearing such headlines as "SALOONS NOT THE CAUSE OF ALL CRIME" and "LIQUOR NOT THE CAUSE OF POVERTY."

Images of the brazenly lawless saloon were furthered by the near universal refusal of large cities to enforce laws requiring saloons to close on Sundays. The Sunday-closing statutes— usually state laws passed by rural-dominated legislatures—

clashed with the majority immigrant, working-class culture of many cities that envisioned Sunday as a day for relaxation and amusement as well as religious duty. "After six days of work and toiling, the Germans want to enjoy life freely on Sunday," explained a defender of the "Continental" Sunday. "Some people will go to the Church in the morning. Many more people will go in the afternoon to theaters and afterwards to cafes and restaurants. Some other people will stay at home or flock to saloons to meet old friends and make new acquaintances." Many immigrants saw no reason to adopt the stern Puritan tradition of "a dead Sunday, with the silence of a graveyard and bare of any joys of life." But for outraged supporters of Sunday closing, the open saloons symbolized the contempt for law and morality that they believed was at the heart of saloon culture.

By sponsoring too many saloons and demanding that they turn a quick profit, brewers contributed to the image of rampant lawlessness in the saloon trade. They were nevertheless shocked to find that the unsavory aura of the saloon undermined their efforts to promote beer as a healthy moderate beverage. Since the mid-nineteenth century, brewers and German immigrants alike had contrasted the wholesome, sociable properties of beer with the dangers of distilled liquor. "Whiskey makes a man ugly and corrupts his stomach," argued a brewing journal in 1880. "Beer, on the other hand, mellows him, links him with the universal brotherhood, superintends a physical and moral serenity, and makes him a friend to his kind." In a viewpoint that echoed the eighteenth-century opinions of Benjamin Rush, some brewers even denied that beer caused drunkenness. "Men drinking beer exclusively may become 'funny' but never drunk," contended a brewer in 1902. Indulgence in distilled liquor, however, had darker, socially disruptive consequences, according to the same observer. "All people hate drunkards," he said, "and whiskey makes them."

But the representation of beer as a pleasant, socially responsible beverage was contradicted by its association with the saloon. For millions of Americans, the saloon conjured up, in the words of Norman Clark, "images of sodden drunks, of hideously fat men sucking stale cigars, of toilets fouled with vomit and urine in the haze of alcoholic narcosis, of the blind idiocy of drunken violence." If beer attracted crowds of men to such repulsive places, asked critics of the saloon, how could it promote health, wholesome fellowship, and social happiness, as the brewers claimed? After hearing from the brewers how whiskey alone promoted intemperance, representatives of the distilled liquor industry were quick to point out the connections between brewers and saloon degeneracy. "Who has encouraged the violation of law and the establishment of low drinking places?" asked the National Liquor Dealers' Association in 1906. "Certainly not the whisky interest. . . . There are very few saloons controlled by the whisky trade." The villains, it clearly implied, were the brewers. Saloons, an economic necessity for the expanding brewing industry, ironically became the principal threat to its survival.

All branches of the beer and liquor industries recognized by 1908 the danger posed to them by unruly or illegal saloons, but mutual hostility among brewers, distillers, and retail dealers prevented a coordinated reform program. By then the prohibition movement had developed into a disciplined political force. The United States Brewers' Association proposed to "stem the tide of prohibition by . . . declaring war against the dives." But the brewers assigned the blame elsewhere for the profusion of "the immoral saloon." They acknowledged "that keen competition has in the past led to a multiplication of saloons beyond the actual requirements of the market," but

credited "the existence of unruly saloons" to disreputable saloonkeepers and "a certain class of politicians who keep them
alive for their own purposes."

Saloonkeepers proved no more eager than the brewers to
accept responsibility for the dismal reputation of their trade.
The Knights of the Royal Arch, a barmen's organization committed to saloon reform, made little headway. Rather than
uniting in order to police themselves, saloonkeepers blamed
industry abuses on others. The objectionable dive, one bar
owner contended, was "typically a brewery saloon." Some embattled saloonkeepers attacked temperance workers and even
their own customers for saloon excesses. "Don't blame the saloonkeepers, ladies," read one reply to WCTU complaints.
"BLAME THE UNGOVERNED AND UNGOVERNABLE BOYS YOU
BRING UP." Unwilling to accept blame for problem saloons, the
industry also was unable to work together to eliminate them.
When the distilled liquor trade advocated a protective program of government saloon regulation called the Model
License League, suspicious brewers held back from participation. Throughout the drive toward prohibition, mutual re-
crimination and the overextended, ruthlessly competitive
character of the retail trade stood in the way of industry efforts to reform the image of the saloon.

Despite bitter rivalries within the drink trade, popular images of a concentrated, monopolistic "liquor trust" run with a
callous disregard of the public interest had become influential
by the turn of the century. State and local combinations of
brewers, distillers, and retailers, whose unity of action often
camouflaged the disarray of the national industry, raised
money and openly engaged in political action to prevent the
passage of prohibition laws. Vigorous lobbying of this kind
suggested the existence of a substantial organized liquor interest. Brewery ownership of saloons, the most visible element of

the corporate reorganization that transformed the liquor business by 1900, furthered the impression that a centralized, well-financed, and greedy cabal of businessmen orchestrated every move within the liquor industry.

The patterns of American business enterprise encouraged belief in the existence of a dangerous liquor trust. The late nineteenth century was a dynamic period of business consolidation, reorganization, and mergers that gave rise to such mammoth corporations as United States Steel and Standard Oil. In an effort to rationalize operations, limit disruptive competition, stabilize costs, and develop secure markets, American manufacturers devised the technique of vertical integration—gaining control of all phases of production and marketing. Corporations acquired raw materials, transportation facilities, factories, and distribution networks. The tied-house system was a dimension of vertical integration in the brewing business. As brewers acted to gain control of the sale of beer, the market share of the largest firms grew. Concentration in the distilling business was accomplished by absorbing individual firms into larger corporations, a process known as horizontal integration. In 1899 the creation of the Distilling Company of America joined the four major liquor combinations, who together produced 90 percent of the nation's distilled spirits. At a time when rapid corporate consolidation prompted fears that monopoly power might override popular democracy, the saloon came to represent a double threat to its anxious critics. Not only was the saloon a breeding ground for crime and social disorder, it was also an extension of an irresponsible yet powerful industry that reached into nearly every American community.

If, as many temperance backers supposed, each saloon was an outpost of the liquor trust, their prominent place in urban political life threatened to corrupt democracy. The connection between the masculine culture of drinking and the masculine domain of politics remained tight as the nineteenth century gave way to the twentieth. Voters in the Progressive Era still expected candidates to treat them to drinks, and saloons, as neighborhood centers, still functioned as political gathering places. Of 1,002 nominating conventions held by the major parties in New York City during a single year, 633 took place in saloons and 96 others met next door to a saloon. During elections in many cities, the back rooms of saloons were still used as polling stations, and party ward heelers gathered the large urban "floating" vote of rootless men together in barrooms before marching them to the ballot box. A sufficient number of saloonkeepers held political office to support the story that a jokester caused a stampede out of the St. Louis municipal assembly by paying a boy to yell, "Mister, your saloon is on fire." The 46-seat Milwaukee city council, for example, in 1902 included 13 saloonkeepers. The saloonkeeper-politician was never as dominant as urban legend had it (Chicago had only 7 liquor retailers among its 70 aldermen in 1900), but public officials connected to the liquor industry retained an influential presence in city politics during the Progressive Era.

Saloons were closely integrated into the mechanics of urban machine politics at election time, but they were also deeply involved in the corrupt flow of money and favors that lubricated the system between elections. Saloons that wished to ignore Sunday-closing laws often had to pay representatives of the local political organization for the privilege. Saloon operators bribed policemen to look the other way while they stayed open all night or ran gaming tables. Unlicensed barrooms, which remained undisturbed much of the year, were assessed annual fines that served as informal business permits. Bogus crews for sham public works projects were recruited in saloons and returned after a day of light or phantom labor to toast their political benefactors over the bar.

Saloons, in short, often functioned as clearinghouses for the underground exchange of money and favors that built loyalty to political machines. In addition, the legitimate revenue from saloon license fees made liquor retailers vital contributors to municipal treasuries. The historian Perry Duis calculated that more than 22 percent of Chicago's operating income in 1906 came from saloon license payments. For both its formal and underground operations, city government at the turn of the century was to some degree obliged to the saloon. As one temperance activist put it, "boodle and booze," the corrupting wares of the political boss and the saloonkeeper, were "diabolical twins" which together threatened to poison American politics and society.

But the image of saloon depravity too easily concealed the more complex role of saloons in immigrant and working-class neighborhoods. This became clear in the 1890s to middle-class social investigators from settlement houses and universities who, under the sponsorship of progressive groups such as the Committee of Fifty to Investigate the Liquor Problem, directly observed saloon culture. They discovered that, aside from dispensing alcoholic drinks, many saloons provided vital services to working-class neighborhoods. Without easy access to banks, many workers cashed their paychecks in saloons and used saloon safes to store valuables. Saloons frequently catered to workers of specific trades, and barrooms often doubled as hiring halls. As one of the few open, public rooms in overcrowded neighborhoods, saloons offered a place to use a telephone, receive mail, read a newspaper, or use a toilet. One observer emphasized that the saloon "furnishes the common lavatory for the entire city."

The free lunch, a feature of saloon life that critics deplored

as a dangerous enticement to drink, was particularly important to many saloon patrons. A product of the wildly competitive atmosphere of the late nineteenth century, the free lunch
offered a complimentary buffet with the purchase of a nickel
beer. Sometimes the fare was meager and salty, clearly intended to provoke thirst, but more often saloons provided
bread, cheese, luncheon meats, hot dogs, clams, eggs, and vegetables. Saloon food was better than that offered by the filthy
five-cent restaurants in working-class districts and was
cheaper than that sold in the ten- and fifteen-cent restaurants.
"All the charity organizations in Chicago combined are feeding fewer people than the saloons," concluded an investigator
from the Chicago Commons settlement.

The most important function of the urban, working-class
saloon, observers agreed, was as "the poor man's club."
Working-class men had no access to the well-appointed hotel
bars and exclusive clubs that offered recreation to salaried and
professional men. For men who worked in sweaty, often dangerous jobs and lived in crowded, stuffy tenements, the saloon
beckoned as a warm, well-lit, pleasant refuge for relaxation
and masculine companionship. Men played cards, read newspapers, discussed politics, sports, and theology in saloons.
Many barrooms provided pool tables or pianos; occasionally
there was an attached gymnasium, bowling alley, or handball
court. Middle-class commentators acknowledged the appeal
of such saloons. While in law school, the reformer Frederic
Howe studied in a saloon across the street from his boarding-
house. "It was the only friendly place in New York for me," he
fondly recalled. "It was my club, where I had a comfortable
warm corner to myself." An investigator from Hull House in
Chicago reported that during his visits to more than two hundred saloons in his working-class ward, "I saw just three
drunken men." Even amidst such amiable fellowship, how-

ever, there were reminders of the objectionable aspects of the male culture of drinking. Another Chicago-based investigator observed that "almost without exception," saloons displayed pictures of naked women, often on the playing cards distributed by the brewers. Boston police tried to prohibit women from entering saloons, reasoning that no females except prostitutes would find the confines of a barroom congenial.

There was, in fact, great variety in the types of drinking places that were known collectively as saloons. In some working-class districts in Boston, for example, saloons were bare rooms without seats in which "drinking is excessive" and "loitering . . . after the drink is finished is not encouraged." Barrooms near the commercial districts in cities were often ornate affairs, with orchestras and restaurants offering business lunches. Saloons in suburban areas attracted more families than city saloons. In a class of its own was the German beer garden, which flourished in leafy suburbs and the occasional urban green oasis. For the entry fee of a quarter, a customer was admitted to an extensive landscaped garden with a bandstand and open-air tables to which waiters brought drinks. Some beer gardens could accommodate several thousand visitors; entire families came for music and dinner. Saloons catering to bicyclists and funeral parties clustered near roads and cemeteries. Many liquor-selling establishments were not properly saloons at all but rather groceries and pharmacies. Finally, many cabarets, dance halls, and private immigrant clubs and ethnic fraternal associations held liquor licenses.

When concerns over saloon criminality and the immorality that accompanied the culture of drinking began to touch on immigrant associations, the effect on urban politics was explosive. The suicide of a Chicago teenager in front of a popular dance hall in 1905 ignited one such outburst. Special liquor licenses issued by the city allowed many dance clubs to serve alcoholic drinks until three o'clock in the morning, two hours later than state law permitted. Newspaper reports had condemned the "drunken orgies" that encouraged unsupervised youths to "learn the way to crime," even suggesting that prostitution rings operated near some of the night spots. After the suicide, state prosecutors demanded that all drinking establishments be closed at 1 a.m., in compliance with state law. Under pressure from state officials, Chicago authorities stopped granting special liquor licenses to private clubs, including ethnic societies and social clubs.

Outraged that their quiet clubrooms had been linked to "the condemned and criminal vice dens," Chicago Germans, Bohemians, Poles, and other immigrant communities quickly took action. A coalition of singing societies, gymnastic clubs, and other associations banded together into a sixty-thousand-member organization called the United Societies for Local Self-Government. Although it was careful to condemn "the abuses and temptations of 'saloon life,'" the United Societies forced a chastened city council to reissue the special liquor permits. The immigrant confederation then turned its attention to the state Sunday-closing law, which angry rural lawmakers now demanded be enforced. Asserting that great cities such as Chicago had "the absolute right to regulate the customs and pleasures of their inhabitants in their own way," representatives of the United Societies forced the Chicago charter convention, which was constructing a badly needed modernization of the city charter, to include proposals giving the city exclusive authority to regulate Sunday closing and the sale of liquor by private clubs, thereby avoiding tighter state standards.

The charter rapidly became a hostage to liquor regulation. State legislators, who had to approve the charter before it was put to a popular vote, objected to the liquor provisions. "I

don't know how a German or a Bohemian would look if he
had to get over a Sunday without a drink," mocked one small-
town representative. The legislature stripped the home-rule
liquor proposals from the charter and refused to pass the remainder of it until Chicago representatives gave their support
to a state local-option bill. The United Societies, claiming to
represent "the sentiment of four-fifths of the voters of our
city," led the opposition to the charter, which in 1907 was
soundly rejected by popular vote. Chicago would suffer from
an outdated framework of government for several more
decades. The United Societies would be a significant force in
city politics for a generation. Such was the unpredictable
power of alcohol as a political issue in the Progressive Era.

Politicians and party organizations in the Progressive Era remained as reluctant as ever to embrace the politics of alcohol
regulation. But other developments at the turn of the century—the indictment of strong drink by respected medical
and social scientific authorities; the focus on the saloon as the
embodiment of the most dangerous aspects of industrialization and business consolidation, urban concentration, and
massive immigration; the rising progressive faith in forceful
action to achieve reform—created an opportunity for a resurgent prohibition movement. The Anti-Saloon League of
America, founded in 1895, made the most of that opportunity.

   The Anti-Saloon League exhibited the modern face of traditional middle-class moral concern in America. By centering
its attention on the saloon rather than the drinker, the ASL
signaled its intention to root out the institutional structure
that supported the culture of drinking. It drew from the organized strength of American Protestantism rather than competing for influence within political parties. With its army of
voters focused on specific pieces of legislation, guided by pro-

fessional managers, backed by its own sophisticated publicity network, flexible in its short-term goals, and committed to a policy of sustained pressure on individual officeholders, the ASL was an extraordinarily effective political lobbying group. Along with the Woman's Christian Temperance Union, the ASL shared some of the characteristics of progressive reformers in the early twentieth century: a combination of religious motivation and social scientific methods, an expressed concern for the health and well-being of children and families, an awareness of the impact of the environment on social problems, the adoption of anti-corporate rhetoric, and a fondness for legislative remedies for social ills. Just as the saloon was the appropriate symbol for the renewed attention to strong drink in modern American life, the Anti-Saloon League symbolized the methods by which twentieth-century Americans intended to find a permanent solution to their long struggle with alcohol.

6

The Anti-Saloon League and the Revival of Prohibition

AT THE END of the nineteenth century, as the liquor industry matured and the urban saloon became the object of urgent scrutiny, the push for state prohibition laws had run out of steam. The flurry of activity in the 1880s had culminated in 1889 with the adoption of prohibition in North and South Dakota. Eighteen years passed before another state went dry. During that slack time, four of the seven prohibition states (Iowa, South Dakota, New Hampshire, and Vermont) again allowed the sale of liquor. Even in the stalwart prohibition state of Kansas, enforcement of the law eased in the 1890s. Illegal saloons were tolerated there if the "joints" were willing to pay regular "fines" to local governments. By this device, saloons operated in the major cities and more than half the counties of the Sunflower State.

The primary organized advocates of prohibition, the Prohibition party and the WCTU, also suffered setbacks. The modest national political influence exercised by the Prohibition party in the 1880s quickly vanished, and with the death of Frances Willard in 1898, its alliance with the WCTU eroded. Without the endorsement of the WCTU, the Prohibition party slipped into the doctrinaire fussiness that commonly afflicted radical fringe organizations. Although on a firmer foundation than the Prohibitionists, the WCTU also staggered under financial mishaps and internal disputes as Willard (and her influence) faded away. Just as the American culture of drinking began to exhibit renewed vitality, the organized temperance movement seemed weak and disoriented.

Despite the sag in prohibitionist fortunes at the turn of the century, the widespread distaste for the saloon presented opportunities for a dry resurgence. Sometimes the resistance to saloons revived the desperate methods of the past. Women's crusades broke out in scattered localities. Isolated outbursts of vigilante action against saloons occurred throughout the 1890s and culminated in 1900–1901 with Carry Nation's notorious hatchet attacks on illegal Kansas barrooms. Elsewhere more innovative means were employed to eliminate saloons. Adopting a practice first tried in Gothenburg, Sweden, the city of Athens, Georgia, in 1891 took over the local liquor trade. City authorities purchased liquor, analyzed it for purity, and sold it to adults (in pint bottles or larger quantities) at a municipal dispensary. The dispensary was closed on Sundays, election days, and holidays. Typical saloon abuses were therefore avoided.

The hope of ending saloon troubles and the promise of government revenue from liquor sales prompted several Georgia counties to follow the lead of Athens and open dispensaries. In 1893 South Carolina governor Benjamin Tillman, in an attempt to bypass popular calls for prohibition, forced the state legislature to install a statewide dispensary system. Laws passed in North Carolina, Alabama, and Virginia between 1895 and 1908 allowed communities in those states to establish local dispensaries as well. Only South Carolina, however, made a full commitment to the dispensary system and thus

"Ben Tillman's baby" became the principal test of an alternative form of liquor control during this period.

But the drawbacks of vigilantism and state ownership of liquor outlets became immediately apparent. Carry Nation's violent actions and bizarre personal behavior lent an unwelcome air of fanaticism and even burlesque to the determined moral activism of American women. Violence also marred the debut of the South Carolina dispensary. Six people died in an 1894 shootout between special state officers empowered by Tillman to enforce the dispensary law and civilians enraged by the lawmen's violation of local sovereignty. State militia units then refused Tillman's order to suppress resistance to the law. Further bloodshed was, with difficulty, avoided, but legal tangles and spreading corruption hampered the system over the next decade. In 1907 the dispensary was scrapped. Neither Carry Nation's hatchet nor Tillman's attempt to impose the dispensary system on a reluctant citizenry adequately tapped the potential force of popular anti-saloon sentiment. To be effective, dry initiatives had to work within the law and respect the limits of public opinion.

In the 1890s scores of local and state temperance societies had learned those lessons. Working through church groups, local WCTU chapters, and other grass-roots associations, dry activists demanded the passage of local option laws and insisted on vigorous enforcement of existing anti-liquor statutes. Together they represented a hidden source of prohibitionist strength during the apparent futility between 1890 and 1906. As state prohibition initiatives languished, local-option laws spread to thirty states. By 1906 more than half the counties, 60 percent of incorporated towns and villages, and close to 70 percent of American townships—territory in which almost 35 million Americans (40 percent of the population) resided—had banned saloons.

Giving coherence to these efforts was the Anti-Saloon League, which grew from a local Ohio society into a national temperance powerhouse through an emphasis on careful organization and realistic, forceful political action. The ASL promoted a new temperance sensibility which shunned the antics of Carry Nation and the hopeless crusades of the Prohibition party. "There is no need for the business man or church member to make street speeches for temperance," reasoned a convert to ASL methods. "I don't believe in fanatics. They do not accomplish what common sense does."

Drawing on the dominant trends of the Progressive Era, the ASL infused organization and professionalism into the prohibition movement. First, it knit together a mass constituency opposed to the liquor traffic—the communicants of the major Protestant churches. Through its paid professional staff, the League then directed that mass sentiment toward the passage of specific pieces of legislation. The League maximized its political influence by rigid attention to the single issue of temperance and its willingness to accept incremental gains. Finally, the League broke through the barrier of party loyalty that hamstrung other temperance groups. Its "omnipartisan" strategy offered support to any officeholder or candidate, regardless of party, who pledged to back its measures. "The League has to do with candidates, rather than parties," a League official reminded nervous party loyalists in its ranks. In short, as Jack Blocker has observed, the Anti-Saloon League was the "prototype of the political pressure group," the first outstanding example of modern interest-group mobilization to influence public policy. Spurred by the efforts of the ASL, prohibition traveled the same path of other Progressive Era reforms, building from local triumphs to state victories to national success.

The Anti-Saloon League was the creation of Howard H. Russell, a lawyer turned Congregationalist minister. As a divinity student at Oberlin College in the mid-1880s, Russell became involved in local efforts to enforce saloon regulations. In 1888, at the behest of the Oberlin Temperance Alliance, he lobbied the Ohio legislature in support of the township local-option law. Called to preach in Missouri in 1890, he organized an Anti-Liquor League there. After a stay at the Armour Mission in Chicago, Russell returned to Oberlin in 1893 determined to mount a more effective fight against saloons. With the aid of the Oberlin Temperance Alliance, he founded the Ohio Anti-Saloon League, gained the endorsement of Ohio Methodist bodies, and soon hired Edwin C. Dinwiddie, Purley Baker, and Wayne Wheeler, all of whom became important national figures in the prohibition movement, to organize the state.

Even though Oberlin was steeped in the anti-slavery tradition of uncompromising moral reform, the leaders of the ASL rejected the inflexible approach of the Prohibition party, many of whose older adherents had ties to the anti-slavery cause. Ten to twelve years younger than their Prohibitionist party counterparts, ASL leaders preached the effectiveness of practical politics. "The 'abolitionists' who fanned the fires of anti-slavery agitation before the war are comparable to the straight-out 'prohibitionists' of today," the League's newspaper later insisted. "Neither accomplished much in practical results."

Taking issue with the position of Prohibitionists and the WCTU, the ASL stressed the value of realistic political compromises to open the road to prohibition. "Temperance people everywhere should take conditions, not as they ought to be," insisted the League, "but as they are." Local-option legislation was the League's preferred device for extending prohibition territory in states unwilling to go completely dry. Local-option elections—referenda in which voters decided whether saloons should be licensed—could be held at the county, municipal, or even precinct level within cities. The ASL found it by far the most flexible legislative method for attacking saloons wherever they were vulnerable.

Although Frances Willard criticized the "half-way measures" of the ASL in 1894, others found its realistic, nonpartisan approach attractive. Members of the Non-Partisan WCTU, Willard's rivals, contributed money to the Ohio League and arranged for Russell to meet with John D. Rockefeller, who soon became an important contributor to the League. In 1895 the Ohio League joined with a similar Anti-Saloon League from the District of Columbia and several other temperance associations to form the American Anti-Saloon League (renamed the Anti-Saloon League of America in 1905). In 1897 the WCTU began cooperating with the ASL. By 1900 the League had formed relationships with influential state temperance associations such as the Kansas State Temperance Union and Indiana's Anti-Liquor League, and had started founding state League affiliates. By 1907 the ASL was at work in forty-three states and territories, sending some 300,000 copies of its journal, *The American Issue*, monthly to its subscribers. In 1909 the incorporation of the American Issue Publishing Company in Westerville, Ohio, allowed the League to supplant the National Temperance Society as the primary publisher of temperance literature in the United States.

The rise of the ASL was directly tied to its claim to act as the agent of organized Christianity in its battle against saloon lawlessness and immorality. At the end of the nineteenth century, several Protestant denominations took forceful stands in opposition to the drink trade. The Methodist Episcopal church urged its communicants to vote against the saloon and those politicians who were in "criminal complicity with the liquor traffic." The temperance committee of the Presbyterian church pushed for the formation of the national ASL in 1895, and in 1900 the Southern Baptist Convention endorsed prohibition. ASL officials, virtually all of whom were ordained ministers or active laymen, welcomed support from the churches. In 1903 the League cemented its alliance with organized Protestantism by restructuring state leagues into church federations. In the federation scheme, each member denomination elected representatives to the board of trustees of state League affiliates. Methodists, Baptists, Presbyterians, and Congregationalists formed the bulk of cooperating churches. Many liturgical confessions, especially Catholic and Lutheran churches, maintained cool and sometimes antagonistic relationships with the League. Nevertheless the ASL advertised itself as "the church in action against the saloon."

Temperance action had traditionally been linked to evangelical Protestantism, but the ASL directed that sentiment down unprecedented channels. Rather than insisting on the election of godly men to office, the League directed its followers to support anyone who backed League measures. League policy called on dry voters to "forsake their party in at least one campaign, and vote for a man who is personally distasteful to them, who does not belong to their church and their lodge, and who stands right, instead of a man on their own party ticket who perhaps belongs to their church, belongs, perhaps, to all their lodges, and is a personal friend, but who stands wrong." Although League members were expected to abstain from alcohol, the organization made no such demands on its political friends. Drinkers and the temperate, Republicans and Democrats, reformers and machine politicians alike were offered electoral help by the League if they voted for its proposals. On the other hand, neither religious nor reform credentials could save lawmakers from League opposition if they blocked dry initiatives. Only the temperance issue mattered, the ASL emphasized, not the party, general outlook, or personal morality of public officials.

The absence of women from the Anti-Saloon League signified another abrupt reversal from recent patterns of temperance reform. The League worked closely with the WCTU, especially in the South, paid tribute to the dry allegiances of American women, welcomed their participation in public demonstrations, and in so far as the single-interest focus of the ASL allowed, offered rhetorical support for the enfranchisement of women; but all League professionals were men. In 1907 General Superintendent Purley Baker declared that women "can do the best service against the liquor traffic through the Church and the Woman's Christian Temperance Union," while men should work through churches and the ASL. Perhaps the League wished to distance itself from the "do everything" reformism of Willard; perhaps it felt its professional orientation and hard-hitting political style were incompatible with the voluntaristic traditions and gentler images of women's activism. Whatever the reasons, ASL officials did not debate the place of women in the League; they simply acted as if the League were self-evidently a men's organization. In practice, the need to drum up temperance votes influenced the direction of League appeals. When critics of the League in Maryland charged that only voteless women attended ASL rallies, the state superintendent illustrated the League's political punch by restricting attendance at the overflow meetings to men.

In order to impose discipline on its followers, the ASL also broke with the more open, democratic organization that had characterized the WCTU and the Prohibition party in the late nineteenth century. K. Austin Kerr, the principal historian of the League, contends that Russell and other ASL architects molded the League's organizational structure so as to duplicate the centralization, bureaucracy, and efficiency of a business. Although representatives of churches and other temperance groups sat on ASL boards, actual control of operations at the state and national levels rested in the hands of salaried superintendents and their professional staffs. Superintendents determined strategy, wrote model bills, fashioned publicity, lobbied legislators, managed fund-raising, and orchestrated the protests and pleas of the League's mass following. Wayne Wheeler, the talented Ohio superintendent, reportedly bragged that he won elections with a minority of voters, "the way the bosses do it. . . . I list and bind [League followers] to vote as I bid."

Men trained in the model Ohio League or in well-organized Illinois fanned out to assume superintendent positions in other states, prompting League loyalists from other regions to complain of the tight circle of "Ohio men" who ran ASL affairs. Although inept and contrary League representatives could be found, especially in the early years of agitation, a core group of talented and like-minded insiders guaranteed continuity in League policies and operations. As if to emphasize the League's departure from temperance traditions, the ASL prospered in the West, Midwest, and South while floundering in New England—the center of mid-nineteenth-century prohibitionist strength.

From its founding until 1913, the Anti-Saloon League concentrated on building strong state organizations, raising public consciousness through a deluge of publicity and agitation, and securing the passage of local and state laws to expel saloons from as much territory as possible. The League's national staff coordinated policy, directed resources, and influenced federal legislation in support of state laws. But to survive, the enterprise required clear demonstrations of effective organization and meaningful political clout. The Ohio League provided a model of workable organization for other states to emulate. It created separate departments to carry on its primary activities: agitation to build public spirit; legislation to prepare laws and lobby for them; law enforcement to keep liquor laws effective; and finance to build a self-sustaining organization.

Ohio League officials drafted a model local-option law to introduce at the 1894 session of the state legislature, printed thousands of copies for distribution, and dispatched organizers across the state to generate enthusiasm for the new association. After the predictable defeat of the model law, the League targeted one prominent opponent of the bill at the next election and ousted him from office. But success did not come rapidly. Instead the League learned to follow a long-term strategy of careful organization and persistent pressure over several legislative sessions. This became the model for League action nationwide.

It took more than a decade for the Ohio League's organizational efforts to pay off. Patient work in the churches yielded lists of temperance voters. By the 1899 campaign, the League had compiled a file of about 100,000 reliable voters to contact and employed 100 field-workers to stir up additional dry votes. Every two years between 1896 and 1904, the League advanced local-option bills in the state legislature, winning some victories but, more important, identifying figures in the Ohio Republican party who were central obstacles to the passage of effective temperance legislation. Despite the fact that Ohio

ASL officials were themselves Republicans, the League took on the GOP.

When Republican governor Myron T. Herrick intervened in 1904 to weaken a bill that would have dried up some sections of Ohio's notoriously wet cities, the League announced its intention to unseat Herrick in the 1905 election. Immediately it launched a publicity campaign against him, urging ASL speakers to act as "prosecutors" against the "Herrick saloons" and the governor who protected them. League pressure secured the nomination of a dry Democrat, John M. Pattison, to oppose Herrick. Then the League raised $73,000 for the campaign, blanketed the state with printed material, and, assisted by the Ohio WCTU, met with voters and urged them to join the fight against "party bossism." Pattison trounced Herrick by almost 43,000 votes to become Ohio's first Democratic governor in nearly fifty years and the only Democrat elected to statewide office that year. Shocked into attentiveness, Ohio legislators enacted major ASL bills in 1906 and 1908, and Ohio Republicans brought the GOP into close cooperation with the League. By defeating a sitting governor in a state with a significant pro-liquor population, and by demonstrating its willingness to cross party lines in pursuit of temperance goals, the Ohio League inspired struggling affiliates in other states and won nationwide respect from watchful politicians.

As it matured, the Anti-Saloon League developed a cagey, even cynical talent for political organization. This was especially evident in its relationship with the churches. Although the League enjoyed the support of several large contributors (Rockefeller donated $5,000 annually after 1904, and S. S. Kresge also gave generously), it relied on small contributions to sustain its operations. That money was gathered at the Anti-Saloon Field Day, an annual event in which cooperating churches devoted one regular Sunday service to work of the

League. In place of sermons, League workers reported on the progress of dry campaigns and then solicited funds, mostly by subscription cards which allowed money to be mailed directly to League headquarters. The ASL demanded full control of the fund-raising process. As an "invariable rule," League representatives refused to enter churches that offered a pulpit but declined a subscription. The League likewise rejected church offerings in lieu of entertaining Field Day speakers, and denied the request of some churches to target their money toward specific projects. Aggressive fund-raising allowed the state leagues to take in nearly $1 million in 1910. That money was plowed back into fieldwork, especially after a 1913 structural change in the ASL redirected money from well-financed states to buttress cash-poor League operations elsewhere.

In many states the League supervised anti-saloon agitation in the churches just as closely as it monitored fund-raising. William H. Anderson, the hard-charging Illinois superintendent, sent a pamphlet to pastors in the state, explicitly instructing them to interrupt revivals if necessary to preach in favor of the League's 1905 local-option bill. The pamphlet also gave tips on dealing with newspapers, warned against statements "so beautifully indefinite that the people will take this for a regular temperance sermon," and stressed that the Anti-Saloon League be mentioned by name. Two thousand clergymen complied with the request. In 1907, again at Anderson's urging, 2,500 pastors spoke in support of the local-option bill, which was enacted into law. That same year 30,000 churches across America participated in a special Temperance Sunday sponsored by the ASL.

Beyond making pastors unofficial League speakers, the close ties the ASL maintained with the churches also produced valuable grass-roots political networks. The church federation in Illinois, for instance, provided an existing infrastructure which facilitated thorough community organization. Voter committees drawn from Protestant youth societies canvassed their congregations and neighborhoods on behalf of League-endorsed candidates. They prepared detailed lists of voters, indicating such items as party preference, attitudes toward particular candidates, and names of influential sympathizers. By using the churches, the Illinois League in 1913 had at its disposal an organization of about 15,000 committeemen, "reaching every county and nearly every precinct" in the state. Even in Pennsylvania, one of the wettest states in the Union, four years of church work up to 1908 provided the state League with a file of 50,000 to 75,000 voters and a fighting chance in the legislature.

Every move the League made during its rise to prominence was governed by practicality. Anderson, in a 1906 manual known within the ASL as the "blue book," emphasized that the League "is sufficiently opportune to seek results." That hard-edged opportunism became the organization's distinguishing characteristic. It influenced sharp decisions on the use of resources. The League hierarchy moved to weed out "the ministerial misfits and clerical flotsam" who staffed some League affiliates and replace them with an "expert working force." After local requests for League assistance in prosecuting liquor-law violations tied down ASL attorneys, the League briskly announced that it was "a moral leader rather than a moral scavenger" and would not furnish detectives or "fritter away" the efforts of its lawyers "upon trifles" when there were laws to be written.

The League also streamlined its lobbying operations. Rather than forwarding lengthy petitions to lawmakers, the League asked its supporters to send personal letters. "A man signs a petition because somebody asks him to," reasoned Anderson, "but he writes a letter because he means business."

Cascades of letters and telegrams from church folk made an impact on legislators eyeing their chances for reelection. Before elections, the League published the results of questionnaires it had mailed to candidates and endorsed those who met its temperance standards. But the League was not interested in hopeless causes. It often stayed out of races that it could not win, and asked its followers to cross party lines only when such a course promised concrete results.

No policy of the League was more opportunistic than its emphasis on eliminating saloons. By 1912 ASL presses were producing forty tons of printed material each month, much of it illustrating the low taxes, serene politics, and booming economies of saloonless territory. By focusing its attention on the liquor traffic, the ASL avoided the controversial question of personal consumption of alcohol. Many Americans, including some Catholic priests and laypeople, who were reluctant to unleash the weight of the law on individual tipplers, nevertheless agreed with United Brethren bishop G. M. Mathews that the saloon was "the deadliest enemy of the American home." They could support political initiatives aimed at suppressing an institution so manifestly "non-patriotic, anti-republican, and disloyal to true American ideals and standards of purity and righteousness." The League's stress on saloons rather than the personal habits of drinkers infuriated the Prohibition party (one Prohibition critic called the ASL the "into-saloon" league), but it also attracted greater public cooperation and made possible more important results.

Equally shrewd was the League's coy stance on prohibition. Its official doctrine identified prohibition as an ultimate goal. "Prohibition prohibits better than regulation regulates," stated the 1906 blue book. "Therefore the LEAGUE stands for Prohibition in those states which have or are ready for such laws."

Meanwhile, local-option campaigns would "train and discipline workers in sufficient numbers to overthrow the [liquor] traffic in state and nation." But in many localities the League concealed its pragmatic intentions for local option and even denied advocating prohibition, insisting instead that it only meant to protect the American principle of home rule by means of majority votes. The League made masterful use of Progressive Era democratic innovations such as the initiative, referendum, and primary elections to advance its goals, yet it labored to block the use of these same methods by wets to roll back dry territory. Eventually, of course, constitutional prohibition denied city populations the exercise of home rule on the liquor question altogether. Practical politics at times led zealous ASL officials to exaggerate their successes, hide their purposes from the public, and manipulate the devices of popular democracy, all in the name of closing saloons.

The novelty of the League's brusque lobbying style, as well as its occasional excesses, prompted many critics. The less discerning charged that ASL officials were insincere tricksters out to steal money from gullible temperance folk. More accurate were complaints that the League's emphasis on the liquor issue, not party allegiance, upended political norms. The ASL "is avowedly and openly a political institution," noted a perceptive journalist in 1909, "yet it has so localized its activities that it works with either or both of the two principal parties, as its best interests dictate. It does not hesitate to change from Republican to Democratic over night." Party leaders and many rank-and-file partisans found such behavior puzzling and dangerous. Equally out of step with experience was the League penchant for issuing direct threats to unfriendly legislators. Democratic loyalists, including drys, were genuinely shocked when William Anderson, by then superintendent of the Maryland ASL, suggested in 1910 that officeholders were "babyish" to "whine" when the League upbraided them for their votes on temperance bills.

The bold lobbying of aggressive League agents frequently brought reprisals against the Anti-Saloon League, but in the long run the new methods proved that the ASL was adjusting to a changed political climate faster than many party professionals. The League's unusually rapid success after 1900 was anchored in deep political shifts. The Gilded Age political system, dominant in the late nineteenth century, had valued party fidelity over policy innovation and therefore locked troublesome drys out of the political mainstream. But this reliable party identification crumbled in the turbulent 1890s. The Anti-Saloon League reflected the emerging public-policy orientation, reform outlook, and adventurous political independence of the Progressive Era. Nowhere was that more apparent than in the South, where the ASL combined with the unique dynamics of Southern progressivism to produce a renewed burst of state prohibition laws between 1907 and 1909, a series of victories that broke through two decades of frustration and after 1914 opened a new round of prohibition gains that would culminate in national prohibition.

The Southern states were thickly populated with evangelical Protestants, and in the nineteenth century, fraternal temperance groups such as the Good Templars had prospered there. The region nevertheless displayed considerable hostility to government-imposed prohibition as a solution to the problems associated with intemperance. Southerners had remained aloof in the 1850s as the Maine Law movement swept across the nation. Several states of the Confederacy imposed prohibition to conserve grain during the Civil War, but those laws fell into disuse with the return of peace. Resistance to federal mandates during Reconstruction, and the post-Reconstruction domination of the South by the Democratic party, reinforced the region's fervent attachment to Jacksonian principles of individualism and a suspicion of government power. As late as 1908 a Southern advocate of prohibition confessed that "the people of the South are the historical partisans of personal liberty. They are naturally opposed to sumptuary laws of any kind." A year before the adoption of statewide prohibition in North Carolina, a prominent leader of the state Anti-Saloon League publicly argued that such a law would be "subversive of the spirit of American institutions," because its enforcement would require an intolerable centralization of government authority. For many Southerners, including some temperance activists, the right to drink was still a vital component of democracy.

Although Southerners were reluctant to embrace prohibition, they were willing in the late nineteenth century to pursue less sweeping restrictions on the operations of the liquor traffic. Tennessee's four-mile law of 1877, for instance, barred saloons from the vicinity of chartered rural schools. Other states had similar statutes that cleared drinking places from areas near churches. Steady pressure from church groups, the WCTU, and, after 1900, the ASL expanded the coverage of such laws and influenced the passage of local-option acts that together dried up most of the rural South. By 1907 more than three-quarters of the counties in eleven Southern states were entirely without saloons. Local option even developed into a potent political force in Kentucky, the center of American bourbon production. There the state legislature passed a limited county-option law in 1906 that drove saloons from county districts; after much political turmoil, in 1912 Kentucky lawmakers extended the coverage of county option to include cities and towns exempted from the 1906 statute.

Until about 1907 the hostility of Southern temperance folk to the liquor traffic was counterbalanced by Southern political culture's respect for the individual rights of white citizens. Nineteenth-century political values dictated that social regulation must not infringe on the liberty of free white men. By contrast, during the Progressive Era, social priorities shifted— from protection of the individual to the advancement of society itself, the common good. The fears and aspirations of white middle-class Southerners active in progressive reform ultimately made state prohibition possible.

Southern progressives at the turn of the century deeply feared that disorder and violence would envelop their region, particularly in the form of racial conflict between black Southerners and lower-class whites. Race riots in Wilmington, North Carolina, in 1898 and in Atlanta—the center of the New South creed of efficiency and order—in 1906 were disturbing indications of a potentially violent future. At this sensitive moment, worried observers charged that the unreformed liquor trade was about to set a torch to the powder keg of racial animosity and violent tendencies that underlay Southern society. In Southern saloons, an informed critic wrote, "to drink means ordinarily to drink whisky, and not at table or in the restraining company of women, but in surroundings the least conducive to moderation and decency. It means, therefore, deplorably often, not merely drunkenness, but rowdyism." The irresponsible sale of alcohol threatened to ruin the progressive drive to raise the level of Southern civilization.

Liquor also allegedly fueled black sexual assaults on white women, a crime that white Southerners focused on with peculiar intensity and abhorrence. The Atlanta riot had been sparked by false rumors of such attacks; press reports that a St. Louis distiller had shipped gin labeled with drawings of half-naked white women to be sold to Southern blacks created a sensation in the South. Middle-class whites expressed the patronizing yet sincere concern that liquor would set poor blacks and poor whites alike at one another's throats. "In any Southern community with a bar-room a race war is a perilously possible occurrence," grimly suggested an Atlanta clergyman. Rapes, retaliatory lynchings, and drink-induced rioting, Southern progressives fretted, would undermine "the sacredness of law" and "the integrity of democracy"—key elements of the orderly, prosperous society that progressives hoped to build.

In much of the nation, progressive opinion on the necessity or even desirability of prohibition was divided. But the distinctive circumstances of the South at the turn of the century helped make prohibition an important component of Southern progressives' program for social improvement. Prohibition, many Southerners came to believe, would not only reduce violent disorder in the South, it would advance prosperity and the rule of law. Most significant, progressives hoped, prohibition would confirm the triumph of the public welfare over the fierce Southern individualism that had in the past retarded the social and material development of the region. As a "self-denying ordinance," crowed one supporter, prohibition "represents the growth of the belief in the solidarity of society." In the insightful words of the historian Dewey Grantham, prohibition acted as an essential "bridge between the old and the new, between those who wanted to reform individuals and those who wanted to reform society." By enacting prohibition, Southern reformer Alexander McKelway argued, white citizens were making a dramatic sacrifice for the social good, setting aside their own "personal liberty ... for the protection of the weaker race from the crimes that are caused by drunkenness, and of both races from the demoralization that follows upon racial crime." Prohibition would signify the new maturity of Southern citizenship, making other reforms possible.

The pathway to state prohibition was cleared by another unique feature of Southern progressivism—the disfranchisement of the great majority of black voters. Seven of the nine Southern states that adopted prohibition between 1907 and 1915 first sharply restricted black suffrage. Even though middle-class blacks often voted for prohibition when given the opportunity, the common assumption among the temperance-minded in the South was that black voters cast their ballots in support of the saloon. That assumption still ruled in Arkansas in 1913, where an ASL-sponsored law required the formal approval of a majority of *white* citizens before towns could license saloons.

But the greatest impact of disfranchisement on Southern prohibition was indirect. During the late nineteenth century, conservative Democratic regimes had manipulated the challenge to white supremacy represented by black suffrage and the Republican party, in order to crush reform initiatives and deflect criticism. Democratic and racial loyalties overrode other concerns, including prohibition. In North Carolina, for instance, "no important phase of liquor regulation could be discussed without first considering the possible effect of such regulation upon the Democratic party." Disfranchisement removed the burden of race from Southern progressive politics, once again allowing, as one Virginian put it, "white men to differ on real issues." Disputed subjects such as prohibition could be discussed without risking accusations of racial treason. Indeed, in the new atmosphere, prohibition became a device for furthering white supremacy rather than one that weakened it. Finally, suffrage restriction allowed the nonpartisan methods of the Anti-Saloon League to operate more freely and effectively in the South.

The ASL played only a small role in the triumph of prohibition in Georgia in 1907 and took no part at all in the adoption of prohibition in Mississippi in 1908, but the League was nevertheless an important force in the Southern prohibition drive. Realizing the opportunity offered by the growth of dry sentiment in the South, ASL national superintendent Purley Baker in 1904 appointed George W. Young of the Kentucky ASL as a special national assistant superintendent to promote the League's Southern work. Young provided practical assistance to Southern League affiliates, even after the funding for his new position ran out. Once established, Southern state leagues welded existing temperance coalitions into effective political units which forced prohibition bills through legislative obstacles. An informed Southern prohibitionist credited the League for contributing "a new sort of propaganda" to Southern temperance reform that "elicited, combined and directed public sentiment successfully."

Between 1907 and 1909, the League's legislative expertise and organizing ability helped enact prohibition in Oklahoma (as part of the new state's original constitution), Alabama, North Carolina, and (amid great political excitement) Tennessee. A powerful League affiliate in Virginia, dominated by Methodist bishop James Cannon, pressured legislators and compromised with the conservative state machine of Democratic senator Thomas Martin until the Old Dominion adopted prohibition in 1914, inaugurating a second wave of Southern prohibition victories. The vigorous efforts of League superintendent Brooks Lawrence returned prohibition to Alabama in 1915 after wets repealed the law in 1911. Reorganized and strengthened League operations pushed prohibition through in Arkansas (1915), South Carolina (1915), and Texas (1918). Adoption of prohibition amendments to the state constitutions of Florida (1918) and Kentucky (1919) rounded out the impressive list of state prohibition triumphs in the South.

The prohibition breakthrough in the South illustrated the dramatic new possibilities for alcohol reform in the twentieth century. Not only had the follies of the saloon trade hardened public attitudes against the liquor traffic everywhere in the nation; approaches toward government in the Progressive Era had changed significantly as well. By 1907 Americans seemed more willing to tolerate government action to protect or advance the public interest. State and federal pure food and drug laws, regulation of women's and children's labor, compulsory school attendance requirements, factory safety and consumer protection laws, and tighter controls on business enterprise all imposed government authority over expressions of personal liberty that, in one way or another, harmed the general welfare. Prohibition was a particularly intrusive expression of the same general tendency. The eagerness of many Southerners, who had been the most defiant partisans of traditional notions of personal liberty in the United States, to justify prohibition as a public necessity underscores the critical shift in opinion after the turn of the century. The patient educational work of the WCTU, ASL, and other dry advocates gave direction to this new sentiment, but the drys did not create it, nor were they alone in promoting the notion of using state authority to carry out the public interest. Prohibitionists took advantage of this context of government activism in pursuit of reform, especially after the Anti-Saloon League came to dominate the dry movement. Although the core values of family and morality that motivated prohibitionists can be traced to their nineteenth-century roots, the twentieth-century prohibition movement, as represented by the ASL, derived its strength from an understanding of the organizational outlook and political mechanics of modernity.

The aftermath of prohibition victories in the South never-

THE ASL AND THE REVIVAL OF PROHIBITION

theless clarified the limitations of dry sentiment and emphasized the need for the Anti-Saloon League to apply greater
pressure on the national government to reinforce state efforts.
Historians of the prohibition movement describe a "plateau"
or "equilibrium" in dry advances at the state level between
1910 and 1912. By that time, saloons had been closed in most
areas where they were vulnerable; hard campaigning would
be necessary to eradicate the liquor industry elsewhere. During those years, local-option advances in some states (among
them California, Washington, and Michigan) were offset by
license victories in others (most notably Ohio and especially
Indiana, where in 1911 saloons returned to forty-six previously dry counties). More critical were a string of statewide
prohibition election defeats. Voters rejected prohibition in
Florida, Oregon, and Missouri in 1910, in Texas in 1911, and
in 1912 in Arkansas. West Virginians added prohibition to
their state constitution in 1912, but the preceding year prohibition had been repealed in Alabama. To the temperance faith-
ful, these were discouraging setbacks after the invigorating
dry advances of 1907–1909.

Several short-term factors, beyond the strong opposition to
saloon-closing from urban areas, contributed to the prohibition setbacks. In Arkansas and Texas, poor decisions by inex-
perienced or untalented local Anti-Saloon League officials
forced ill-timed prohibition votes before public opinion had
been adequately cultivated. Assistance from the national ASL
eventually reformed the Texas League and helped the Arkansas League achieve prohibition in 1915. A second reason for
the slowdown of prohibition momentum was the desperate
action of brewers and distillers, who funneled support to local
wet personal-liberty leagues or revamped their own lobbies to
influence state legislatures. Reflecting the heightened activism
of the drink trade, the liquor industry's Model License League

in 1910 helped form the Greater Oregon Home Rule Association. The Ohio Brewers' Association matched the Ohio ASL in political sophistication for a time, and in Texas brewers and distillers joined together in an unprecedented alliance to beat back the threat of prohibition. This too proved temporary, at least at the national level. By 1915 the persistent animosity between brewers and distillers had again disrupted united action on the part of alcoholic beverage producers.

Finally, and most important for future dry strategy, the comparative weakness of the Anti-Saloon League's national legislative wing, along with internal disputes that plagued the organization between 1907 and 1911, hampered the passage of national statutes intended to complement state prohibition laws. Both the courts and Congress were reluctant to tamper with interstate shipments of liquor into prohibition states, a touchy point of constitutional law. Most prohibition states permitted mail orders of liquor for personal consumption but strictly forbade shipments intended for retail sale. Congressional hesitancy to interfere with interstate commerce, however, allowed liquor that stocked illegal barrooms to leak into dry states and thus bolster the wet claim that "prohibition doesn't prohibit." In 1911 alone, the Interstate Commerce Commission estimated that shipping companies delivered more than twenty million gallons of strong drink into prohibition territory. A decisive national dry political presence was necessary to choke off this traffic and restore confidence to local prohibitionists.

Since 1899 the Anti-Saloon League had maintained a national legislative office in Washington, D.C. Its legislative superintendent was Edwin Dinwiddie, a former Prohibitionist who had helped build the Ohio ASL. Together with WCTU lobbyists, Dinwiddie established relationships with congressmen and skillfully used the areas of federal responsibility for liquor—Indian affairs, the military, liquor taxes—to further the dry agenda. At the turn of the century the League and the WCTU curtailed liquor sales on military bases, pushed for greater enforcement of liquor restrictions on Indian reservations, and lobbied Congress to ban saloons in the District of Columbia. But the federal liquor tax—which led government agents to comb the backwoods for illegal stills, supervise the operations of distilleries, and identify all liquor producers and retailers—became an important weapon in the ASL strategy of pursuing "concurrent" state and national action against the liquor traffic. As the historian Richard F. Hamm has demonstrated, unlike earlier temperance groups that viewed the federal liquor tax as a noxious alliance between government and the liquor trade, the League instead used the federal tax as a device to help enforce state and local prohibition. The League sought to use tax information to identify and prosecute liquor-law violators; in 1906 Dinwiddie helped secure a law from Congress that allowed state and local law enforcement officials access to the list of federal liquor tax payers, thus identifying illegal dealers. Although limited in its Washington resources, the League's federal policy seemed adept and creative.

Then things briefly fell apart for the ASL's national office. Dinwiddie feuded with Superintendent Purley Baker and in 1907 resigned his post. He joined a rival temperance alliance supported by the Prohibition party, the Inter-Church Temperance Federation, and established a separate lobby that worked at cross-purposes from the Anti-Saloon League. Weakened by the internal bickering, and frustrated by the resistance of congressional leaders to ASL pressure for restrictions on the interstate shipment of liquor, the League committed a political blunder that further hindered its immediate effectiveness. Joseph Cannon, the despotic Republican

Speaker of the House from Illinois, had used his power to smother interstate liquor regulation; in 1908 the ASL announced that it would attempt to defeat him for reelection to the House. The effort failed and hurt the League among Republicans. Meanwhile Dinwiddie cooperated with Cannon and won support for a 1909 law that tightened regulations on COD (cash on delivery) shipments of liquor. Thrashing wildly, the ASL then decided to work with Cannon as well, just as insurgent Republicans reduced the Speaker's power and the Democrats won control of Congress. Chastened, in 1911 the League made its peace with Dinwiddie (who returned to the League but never regained his earlier influence), closed ranks, and focused on giving dry states the authority to fight liquor shipments from outside their borders.

The result was the most significant national dry victory yet, the passage in February 1913 of the Webb-Kenyon Act. Returning to a winning pattern, the League and the WCTU in 1912 organized a systematic publicity campaign in support of the bill, which barred entry of liquor into any state if the alcohol was to be "in any manner used . . . in violation of any law of such state." This wording allowed the League to portray the act as a state's rights bill—it did not impose federal control on the states but merely allowed state prohibition laws to function without interference. Southern opinion, which for decades had denounced as high-handed the raids conducted on moonshiners by federal revenue agents, and had viewed the expansion of federal controls with deep suspicion, was thus placated. On the other hand, friends of the bill claimed that the proposal maintained congressional authority over interstate commerce, thereby safeguarding constitutional strictures. Both houses of Congress passed the bill with large majorities. Outgoing president William Howard Taft, a constitutional traditionalist, vetoed the law as an unwarranted intrusion of the states into interstate commerce, but Congress easily overrode the veto.

The Webb-Kenyon Act was the very model of concurrent federal legislation that would bolster state prohibition. Not only did the act recharge state prohibition movements, but the passage of the law over Taft's veto, and League national attorney Wayne Wheeler's successful defense of Webb-Kenyon's constitutionality before the Supreme Court in 1917, demonstrated the enhanced power of the Anti-Saloon League in Washington. More significant federal legislation was now possible.

In late 1913 the Anti-Saloon League made the momentous decision to seek a prohibition amendment to the United States Constitution. The liquor forces were again disorganized, and the adoption of the national income tax in 1913 had eliminated the financial justification of licensing saloons. Temperance leaders saw that state agitation alone could not dry up the country. At first the League counseled its followers to settle in for a long struggle, one that possibly would require twenty years of steady labor. Just four years later Congress submitted the 18th Amendment to the states for ratification. It was duly ratified by January 1919 and became effective one year later. The speed with which national prohibition was adopted testified to changed circumstances. It also underlay the enforcement problems that later dogged prohibition and made possible its sudden overturn.

7

War and the Politics of National Prohibition

POLITICAL CIRCUMSTANCES within the United States between 1913 and 1919 hastened the adoption of national prohibition, but those circumstances were deeply influenced by international events. The confidence of American dry activists was bolstered by a parallel stream of anti-liquor policies enacted by other nations. Meanwhile, the possible political consequences of further unrestricted European immigration to the United States caused the Anti-Saloon League to accelerate its push for a national prohibition amendment. Finally, American intervention into World War I significantly aided the swift adoption of prohibition. The pressures of wartime patriotism discredited and silenced German brewers and beer supporters, who had been among the most effective opponents of the dry advance. The pervasive atmosphere of sacrifice and attention to resource conservation that accompanied the American war effort also led to measures that shut down the wartime liquor industry, thus removing another obstacle to prohibition. The wartime emergency further encouraged the expansion of national government authority and emphasized the importance of unity, both of which eased the way for the 18th Amendment through Congress and state legislatures.

During the brisk march to national prohibition, the Anti-Saloon League proved itself supple and potent as a political force. Rather than allowing the war to overshadow the liquor issue, the League used the war to strengthen the case for national prohibition and to lash Congress into stern action against the drink trade. But once prohibition had been achieved, the League came up against its own limitations as a pressure group. Forceful and effective as an advocate for legislation, the League stumbled badly in its attempt to guide enforcement of the prohibition laws. By 1927 the hollowness of the prohibition victory had become as much a part of the League's legacy as the new style of interest-group politics it had pioneered at the turn of the century.

It was helpful to the drys that the American drive toward prohibition took place within a context of ever tighter government regulation of liquor in Europe and North America. Controversial initiatives in Great Britain to restrict the issuance of liquor licenses were reinforced by the outbreak of World War I in 1914, which led the government to regulate the operating hours of public houses and even impose prohibition in some areas of the nation. Popular anti-liquor movements in Scandinavia led in 1919 to the adoption of prohibition in Finland and a ban on hard liquor in Norway, followed in the early 1920s by a government takeover of Sweden's liquor industry. Canadian provinces matched the prohibition gains of American states after 1915 until Canada went completely dry by 1919. Ernest H. Cherrington, chief of publications for the Anti-Saloon League, secretary of the ASL executive council, and one of the League's top strategists, was so taken with the prospect of a dry world that in 1918 he arranged for the organization of the World League Against Alcoholism one year before the ratification of the 18th

Amendment. The worldwide movement to muzzle the liquor trade not only encouraged American temperance advocates to strike boldly, it also suggested to less committed observers that prohibition was in keeping with the modern temper of forward-looking government, not a misguided adherence to outmoded values.

Immigration, a second international force, played a more decisive role in prohibitionist strategy between 1913 and the ratification of the prohibition amendment. Senior ASL leaders such as Howard Russell and Purley Baker had envisioned a lengthy struggle before constitutional prohibition was achieved. Yet Cherrington, upon whom fell the responsibility for planning the campaign, saw the need for swift action. His evenhanded, studious approach to temperance reform stood in marked contrast to the aggressive, self-promoting style of Wayne Wheeler, who became the League's master lobbyist and most celebrated public figure, but both men were political realists. Cherrington knew that state prohibition campaigns could not dry up large urban concentrations of immigrant and working-class Americans. Federal action was necessary, but most drys conceded that Congress did not have the power to force statutory prohibition onto the states. Constitutional prohibition, which required the consent of thirty-six of the forty-eight states, allowed drys the opportunity to outflank the most implacable wet strongholds.

Cherrington believed that many years of temperance education among immigrants and the working class were needed before constitutional prohibition would be fully effective, but he nevertheless pushed for passage of a prohibition amendment within five to seven years. As the historian Austin Kerr has noted, the political impact of immigration quickened the ASL timetable. Between 1910 and 1919, well over six million immigrants entered the United States, most of them before

World War I sharply reduced the flow of newcomers. The great majority of those immigrants settled in cities. Cherrington feared that if the League did not force a prohibition amendment through Congress before the results of the 1920 census were known, congressional reapportionment would increase the number of urban representatives in the House and perhaps deny prohibitionists the two-thirds majority necessary for the passage of constitutional amendments. Alerted by Cherrington's dire prophecy, the ASL resolved to elect a Congress dry enough to pass a prohibition amendment in 1918 or 1920 at the latest.

The League opened the campaign in Washington on a cold day in December 1913 with a public demonstration of dry unity and resolve. "Grand committees" from the ASL and the WCTU joined other temperance workers, many of them grey veterans of dry agitation, in a parade of four thousand marchers down Pennsylvania Avenue to the Capitol. There they presented a prohibition resolution (drafted by a team of ASL lawyers and officials, which included Wheeler and Baker) to Democratic senator Morris Sheppard of Texas and Congressman Richmond P. Hobson of Alabama, a naval hero from the Spanish-American War and an outspoken foe of "the great destroyer" alcohol. The two men had agreed to introduce the measure in their respective chambers. Neither resolution passed that session, but the House offered hope to prohibitionists in December 1914 by supporting Hobson's resolution by a small majority, 197 to 190.

Behind the pageantry, the League's political machinery whirred. League strategists looked past the Sheppard and Hobson resolutions, which they viewed as yardsticks to measure congressional sentiment, to the 1914 elections. As Wheeler later recalled, the League aimed to increase the number of dry senators, vowed to contest every House seat "where

[a] reasonable chance of winning seemed to present itself," and proposed to strengthen the foundation for national prohibition with "an intensive drive back in the States for new dry territory." During 1914 League speakers crisscrossed the country, League petitions and telegrams piled up on the desks of elected officials, and the League spent a record $2.5 million. In the final months of the campaign, Cherrington's presses turned out ten tons of printed material daily, and as many as fifty thousand trained League speakers rallied dry voters in local, state, and congressional races.

The political results in 1914 encouraged the League. State prohibition spread deeper through the South and into the West. Virginia, Oregon, Washington, Colorado, and Arizona adopted prohibition in 1914, all by popular vote. The following year five more states went dry: Alabama (for the second time); Arkansas, Iowa, and Idaho by legislative action; and South Carolina by popular referendum. The Senate was securely dry after the 1914 elections, but the prohibitionist bloc in the House had not increased enough to stretch the Hobson resolution's tiny House majority of 1914 to the two-thirds approval necessary to send a constitutional amendment back to the states for ratification.

Following its finely honed incremental strategy, the ASL set to work on the next campaign. "All the energy we put into the 1914 election boiled and bubbled with hotter fire in the campaign of 1916," observed Wheeler. That fiery energy produced further prohibition victories. Four more states adopted prohibition in 1916, including Michigan, the first major urban, industrial state to go dry. Seattle and Spokane, cities that had rejected the successful Washington prohibition referendum of 1914, returned strong prohibition majorities which helped defeat a 1916 repeal movement. With the 1916 election, the critical dry majority in the House of Representatives had grown by 85 votes over the 197 cast in 1914 for prohibition. "We knew," declared Wheeler, "that the prohibition amendment would be submitted to the States by the Congress just elected." In an extraordinary rush of activity, the ASL had made possible national prohibition.

The League's adept handling of political parties and selective use of pressure aided the quick victory. Before 1916 the League did not force the national parties to take a stand on prohibition. Nor did it demand binding declarations from presidential candidates. Instead the ASL worked to "make it safe for a candidate to be dry" inside both major parties and managed to build significant bipartisan prohibitionist sentiment. Internally divided over the liquor question, Democrats and Republicans maintained official silence on the issue.

Once the League constructed dry majorities in Congress, however, it called for official platform declarations in favor of prohibition. This challenge encouraged the national party organizations, in Austin Kerr's description, "to remove the issue [from partisan debate] by voting for submission" of the prohibition amendment to the states, thereby allowing local representatives to decide the question. By similar adroit maneuvers, the historian Andrew Sinclair noted, the League nudged presidents and party leaders as diverse as Theodore Roosevelt, William Howard Taft, Charles Evans Hughes, William Jennings Bryan, and Woodrow Wilson along a public course from "silence, equivocation, moderate support [to] eventual wholehearted backing of the prohibitionists." It was a measure of the League's political skill that it used the partisan interests of politicians to advance a cause that the party system had steadfastly evaded for half a century.

There was, however, an underlying weakness in the League's national prohibition strategy. The League had built prohibition sentiment by focusing on the perfidy of saloons and the liquor industry rather than the personal use of alcoholic beverages. The structure of state prohibition laws that the League had overseen also made distinctions between the liquor industry and the personal, private consumption of strong drink. Only a handful of prohibition states in 1916 had "bone-dry" laws that outlawed the personal possession and use of liquor. Most others allowed periodic importation or home manufacture of various alcoholic beverages for personal use. In Michigan, as the historian Larry Engelmann has pointed out, prohibition was carried by the votes of "drinking drys," moderate drinkers who saw the need to restrain saloons and the liquor traffic. Drinking drys were an important element of the anti-liquor alliance in many states. Although some members of the dry coalition advocated strict bone-dry laws, the Anti-Saloon League opposed such legislation, fearing it might undermine popular support for prohibition.

In keeping with that position, the Hobson and Sheppard resolutions that the League put before Congress in 1913 barred the manufacture and sale of alcoholic beverages, but not their use. When the Senate in late 1916 added to the Sheppard resolution a ban on personal use of alcohol, the League abruptly dropped its support of the measure and chose to wait for the new Congress before renewing the push for the prohibition amendment. But the logic of national prohibition forced open the question of personal consumption. As Richard Hamm has argued, distinctions between prohibiting the drink trade and prohibiting personal use of liquor that made sense on the state level—where interstate shipments could supply the needs of individual drinkers in prohibition states—collapsed at the federal level. National prohibition would wipe out the American alcoholic beverage industry, leaving only inadequate sources of supply such as home manufacture or importation for individual drinkers.

In February 1917 an unexpected challenge compelled action on the matter of personal drinking before the dry forces had developed a firm, united stance on the feasibility of bone-dry laws. As a dry bill meant to curb liquor advertisements through the mails made its way through the Senate, Senator James Reed, a determined wet from Missouri, attached an amendment that banned interstate shipments of liquor (except for sacramental, medicinal, and industrial uses) into prohibition territory, thus making all prohibition states bone dry, even if their own laws did not require it. Reed's amendment was a "joker," intended to cripple prohibition and damage the Anti-Saloon League, but it became part of the bill passed by the Senate on February 15 and sent on to the House.

Stunned League officials, who had not anticipated Reed's thrust, now faced a dilemma. On the one hand, hard-liners in church groups, the WCTU, and the Prohibition party welcomed the Bone Dry amendment. To oppose it could open a rift in the dry coalition. On the other hand, the League worried that support for the amendment would offend the states' rights sensibilities of Southern prohibitionists and alienate moderate dry opinion elsewhere. With impressive composure, the League withheld an official endorsement of the bill and urged House members to vote as their consciences dictated. When directly questioned by a congressional representative, however, ASL officials James Cannon and Arthur J. Barton, both Southerners, added that their personal convictions favored the Bone Dry amendment. With much commotion, the House on February 21 then passed the Reed amendment, 321 to 72.

The League had boldly turned the trick on the crestfallen Reed, but by doing so it also gambled that public opinion would support a sterner form of prohibition. In the short run the gamble paid off. The League asked states to pass bone-dry measures that would supplement the national law, and by the end of 1917 eighteen states had done so. But the long-run consequences of the bone-dry initiative were unclear. The League itself had not taken the time to clarify its position on the personal use of alcohol; it had merely executed a skillful response to a sudden event. Moreover, the depth of public support for bone-dry prohibition could not be measured by the quick accumulation of state bone-dry statutes in 1917 and 1918. By that time the United States was at war with Germany, and the unpredictable dictates of patriotic enthusiasm had overtaken the nation.

World War I was the greatest of the international influences that shaped the fortunes of prohibition. "The war did three things for prohibition," the historian Charles Merz crisply stated in 1930. "It centralized authority in Washington; it stressed the importance of saving food; and it outlawed all things German." Even before the United States declared war on Germany in April 1917, the European conflict worked to the advantage of the drys. As early as 1915, advocates of American military preparedness demanded a national commitment to efficiency, alertness, and order—all of which, drys pointed out, were incompatible with the use of alcohol. Once the United States entered the war, Congress mandated liquor-free zones around military camps.

More critical to the fortunes of the liquor trade was the damage done by the war to the National German-American Alliance, an ethnic association that since 1901 had actively worked against prohibition. German-American Alliance speakers were outspoken in their support of Germany in the early years of the war. As American relations with Germany worsened after the sinking of the *Lusitania* in 1915, prominent figures such as Theodore Roosevelt and President Woodrow Wilson questioned the loyalty of "hyphenated Americans," especially German-Americans. "A man who thinks of himself as belonging to a particular national group in America has not yet become an American," warned Wilson—with the German-American Alliance in mind.

The sudden unpopularity of the German-American Alliance threatened to drag the brewing industry down as well. In 1913 the United States Brewers' Association, anxious to support a wet lobby not officially tied to producers of alcoholic beverages, began secretly to fund the Alliance. Newspaper reports in 1916, which surfaced just as court cases involving political corruption on the part of brewers in Texas and Pennsylvania were also in the news, accused the Alliance of pro-German activities and the USBA of subsidizing disloyalty. With the enthusiastic approval of the ASL, a congressional investigation of the German-American Alliance laid bare its relationship with the brewers' lobby. In 1918 Congress revoked the charter of the German-American Alliance, and the organization disbanded. As popular denunciation of "the Hun" grew shriller with American entry into the war, the brewers' missteps allowed hyperpatriots to condemn "Pabst, Schlitz, Blatz, and Miller" as "treacherous . . . German enemies" of the United States. In the superheated atmosphere of wartime, brewers and their saloons were transformed from metaphorical into literal enemies of the republic.

American participation in World War I further devastated the liquor trade as it allowed the Anti-Saloon League to recast prohibition into a war issue. Beyond the demonization of German brewers and the desire to keep soldiers in sober fighting trim, the war offered drys a constitutional loophole that hurried along the practical adoption of national prohibition. Under normal conditions, most observers agreed, individual states retained the right over Congress to enact or reject prohibition statutes. But in wartime Congress was granted legisla-

tive authority over matters normally reserved to the states. To
the intense irritation of Woodrow Wilson, who felt that aggressive ASL lobbying hampered his freedom to run the war,
the League resolved to take advantage of expanded congressional war powers to enact stringent national dry legislation.
"If an emergency, by opening a short cut . . . enables the doing
of certain desirable things with less delay and less friction than
would be possible under normal conditions, that is one of the
compensations of such a catastrophe as war," reasoned the opportunistic William Anderson. One "short cut" the League
pursued was a wartime prohibition statute that would dry up
the nation before constitutional prohibition was fully in place.

Wilson summoned the dry Congress elected in 1916 into
special session in April 1917 to declare war against Germany.
At the same time prohibitionists launched what they hoped
would be the final battle against alcohol. The League arranged for its constitutional prohibition amendment to be introduced at the start of the session but then turned its focus to
wartime suppression of the liquor traffic. Heightened attention to the conservation of strategic resources served as an
entry point for the dry lobby. Prompted by the German block-
ade of Britain and France, and anxious to demonstrate a national spirit of sacrifice, the Wilson administration asked for
authority to regulate the production of food and fuel.

With the question "Shall the many have food, or the few
have drink?" drys pressed for the shutdown of the brewing
and distilling industries, both of which used grain in the production of alcoholic beverages, as part of the Lever food-
control bill. In August Congress enacted a version of the
Lever bill that banned the use of foodstuffs in the production
of distilled liquor from September until the end of the war,
thus dismantling the distilling industry. Beer was temporarily
saved by the appeals of labor unions, threats by wet senators to

delay the Lever bill unless beer and wine were exempted from mandatory controls, Wilson's demands for compromise, and the brewers' quick-footed abandonment of the distillers, once more dividing the alcoholic beverage trades in the face of dry pressure. The new law, however, did give the president power to lower the alcoholic content of beer, and in December 1917 Wilson exercised it, reducing the alcohol in beer to 2.75 percent and slashing the grain allotment for brewing by 30 percent.

Finally, on November 21, 1918, after the end of the war and against Wilson's wishes, Congress passed the Wartime Prohibition Act, which banned the manufacture of wine and beer beginning in May 1919 and prohibited the sale of all intoxicating beverages after June 30, 1919, until the end of demobilization, a vague termination point that in practice was delayed until the 18th Amendment became effective. "The average member of Congress is more afraid of the Anti-Saloon League than he is even of the President of the United States," commented a journalist after the lopsided vote. Wilson also recognized the power of the League (and the Republican congressional victories in the recent election) and signed the bill into law. By this measure, national prohibition commenced before the 18th Amendment was even ratified.

Constitutional prohibition nevertheless was the central achievement of the wartime dry surge and the culmination of nearly a century of temperance reform. The speed with which that milestone was achieved sharply contrasted with the long history of the anti-liquor movement. It reflected instead the vigorous pace exhibited by the Anti-Saloon League over the preceding decade. Buoyed by the positive reaction to the Reed bone-dry amendment, additional gains in prohibition territory (four more states went dry in 1917, including the onetime wet bastion Indiana, and Congress voted out saloons in the

District of Columbia in March 1917), and the lockstep patriotism generated by the war, the League made its 1917 prohibition amendment more restrictive than the 1914 Sheppard or
Hobson resolutions. Those earlier measures sought to forbid
the manufacture and shipment of liquor for purposes of sale;
the 1917 version barred the manufacture, sale, and transportation of intoxicating liquor "for beverage purposes." Sensing
more permanence in the rise of bone-dry sentiment than caution warranted, dry leaders believed it safe to outlaw home
manufacture of alcoholic drinks and importation for personal
use. For the second time in 1917, the Anti-Saloon League
stepped beyond its longstanding reluctance to interfere with
individual drinkers.

A series of trade-offs with wet legislators (partly engineered
by Senator Warren G. Harding, a confirmed drinker) yielded
a formula for the adoption of the prohibition amendment. To
be viable, the amendment had to be ratified within seven years
of its submission to the states. A one-year lag between the date
of ratification and the implementation of prohibition would
allow those in the liquor business time to wrap up their affairs
(the Wartime Prohibition Act largely negated this concession).
Following the League's preference, the amendment called for
"concurrent" legislation by the states and the federal government to enforce prohibition. On December 22, 1917, while the
war still raged, Congress approved the prohibition amendment to the Constitution and sent it to the states for ratification. On January 16, 1919, the Nebraska legislature became
the thirty-sixth state body to ratify the 18th Amendment, and
prohibition became part of the Constitution. (All but two
states—Connecticut and Rhode Island—eventually ratified
the amendment.) Wets and drys alike were surprised by the
speed of the outcome. "We thought it would take three or four
years to get the amendment ratified," confessed an ASL offi-

cial. "Instead, . . . the thing's becoming as simple as 'A.B.C.'"
Once more, quick action prevented more extended considera-
tion of the practical consequences of national bone-dry prohibition.

Potential trouble marred the superficial ease of the prohibition victory. Fourteen states, including Illinois, California,
Pennsylvania, New York, and virtually the entire Northeast
from Massachusetts to Delaware, had refused to pass state
prohibition laws. Their ratification of the 18th Amendment
gave no assurance that the cooperation required for the "concurrent" enforcement of prohibition by states as well as the
federal government would be forthcoming. During the
process of ratification there was also some dispute as to what
precisely had been prohibited. Both the 18th Amendment and
the Wartime Prohibition Act had outlawed "intoxicating"
beverages, but neither defined what constituted an intoxicating level of alcohol. In some cities, brewers continued to produce the 2.75 beer that Wilson had decreed for wartime use,
arguing that such a small percentage of alcohol was not intoxicating. Many Americans were shocked in October 1919 when
the Volstead Act, passed after the ratification of the 18th
Amendment to establish enforcement guidelines for prohibition, adopted an arbitrary Internal Revenue Service measure-
ment for taxable alcoholic beverages—0.5 percent—as the
standard for intoxicating liquor, thus prohibiting virtually all
alcoholic drinks. Acting in defiance of the Volstead Act, the
legislatures of New York, New Jersey, and Massachusetts
passed laws in 1920 allowing the production and sale of low-
alcohol beer or light wines. Later that year, in the National
Prohibition Cases, the Supreme Court crushed these local attempts to set alcohol limits higher than those imposed by the
Volstead Act.

The Volstead Act reflected the tighter standards for prohi-

bition favored by the ASL's Wayne Wheeler. From 1919 until
he dropped dead from a heart attack in 1927, Wheeler was the
most influential private citizen in the United States in matters
concerning prohibition. Brilliant and tireless as a dry cam-
paigner, Wheeler was also attracted to power and became
known as the League's key "exponent of force." He had "an
instinct for preeminence," as his publicity secretary put it. He
went so far as to collect, reprint, and distribute press accounts
of his actions as the nation's foremost "legislative bully." More
important, Wheeler overwhelmed his more cautious or ideal-
istic rivals within the ASL and successfully promoted an aggressive enforcement strategy that relied on his fierce skills as
a lobbyist. Ernest Cherrington had been the pivotal figure in
the campaign for constitutional prohibition, but he lost influence to Wheeler after ratification. Once a Republican Congress was elected in 1918, the Republican Wheeler replaced
James Cannon, a Democrat, as the League's chief legislative
official in Washington.

Unlike Cherrington's vision of a gentle introduction to prohibition, with an extensive educational program intended to
wean Americans from their cultural reliance on strong drink,
Wheeler advocated a stringent code of law and rigid enforcement. His approach aimed to make the most of the League's
established political influence. Wheeler furnished lawmakers
with a model bill based on state prohibition regulations, which
Minnesota representative Andrew Volstead revised, steered
through Congress, and helped pass on October 27, 1919, over
the fruitless veto of Woodrow Wilson, then in seclusion after
suffering a debilitating stroke.

The Volstead Act contained three main parts. The first of
these, Title I, added several stringent features to the Wartime
Prohibition Act and clarified its enforcement procedures. (It
was this portion of the act that prompted Wilson's veto.) Title

III established guidelines for the control of industrial alcohol, a vital product in the rapidly expanding chemical industry. Title II imposed the strict 0.5 percent alcohol standard for illegal liquor and set the rules for national prohibition. It assigned responsibility for enforcing the law to the commissioner of the Internal Revenue Service, who worked in the Treasury Department.

The commissioner's agents, set up as the Prohibition Unit (later renamed the Prohibition Bureau) with its own director, were granted considerable powers to combat the traffic in illegal liquor. They were authorized to seize and sell cars, boats, airplanes, and other private vehicles that had been used to carry illegal liquor. They could obtain court injunctions to close for up to one year places where liquor was manufactured or sold; this provision, popularly known as the "padlock law," was one of the most effective enforcement tools during national prohibition. "Bootleggers" (those who manufactured, transported, or sold illegal liquor) could be fined up to $1,000 and jailed for six months for a first offense, with more severe punishment (a maximum fine of $10,000 and five years in jail) for additional violations of the prohibition laws.

The Volstead Act also placed limitations on the strict enforcement of prohibition. Some of these reflected the desire of the Anti-Saloon League to sidestep entangling controversies. The touchy matter of religious freedom was avoided by exempting sacramental wines from the ban on beverage alcohol, although permits were required in order to obtain communion wine. Permits were also granted for the medicinal use of alcohol and for its use in the commercial manufacture of cider and vinegar. Other departures from total prohibition, however, were the result of political compromises that fell short of Wheeler's exacting standards. The most important of these was the personal use exemption.

Wheeler hoped to outlaw the personal possession of strong drink, but Congress offered protection for the possession and use of alcohol in private residences "provided such liquors are for use only for the personal consumption of the owner ... and his family ... and of his bona fide guests." Moreover, Congress blocked searches of private dwellings unless illegal liquor had been sold inside them. Finally, lawmakers added a strange provision to the act that permitted the manufacture of "nonintoxicating" cider and fruit juices for home use, which, given the ban on residential searches, essentially sanctioned the production of homemade wine and hard cider. This provision offered unexpected relief to the California wine industry, which sold grapes and jellies that eager hobbyists easily converted into wine; but it outraged urban beer fanciers who claimed that the law protected the alcoholic drinks of country folk while it banned the favorite beverage of city dwellers. Surprisingly strict in some features and unexpectedly lenient in others, the Volstead Act presented a flawed blueprint for the enforcement of national prohibition.

Shaped by the give and take of congressional politics, the peculiarities of the new law also indicated a disabling weakness in the ASL approach to temperance reform—a weakness that would hobble the enforcement of prohibition and ultimately doom it to failure. Since the turn of the century, the single-issue, bureaucratic orientation of the League and its intense engagement in politics had produced a succession of impressive legislative triumphs for dry reformers, building from local ordinances to state laws until the achievement of national prohibition. But beginning with the Volstead Act, the League's political methods interfered with the successful implementation of prohibition in four related ways.

First, Wayne Wheeler, in a bid to become the power broker of prohibition, overplayed the League's political hand in a manner that damaged the nonpartisan reputation of the ASL and hampered enforcement of the prohibition laws. Second, the passage of the Volstead Act effectively took the liquor issue out of politics. Congressmen and state legislators praised the prohibition laws but quietly withheld the funds necessary for their effective enforcement. Third, the smiling suffocation of prohibition attracted no great public outcry because the enthusiastic backing of the Anti-Saloon League dissipated after the passage of the Volstead Act and the ratification of the 18th Amendment. Success muffled the voice of the prohibition movement in the 1920s and paralyzed the ability of the Anti-Saloon League to force legislators out of their calculated inaction. Popular disappointment in the results of prohibition was the fourth unwanted product of the League's activism. For more than a generation relentless League propaganda had foretold the great social progress that prohibition would inaugurate. Inflated expectations not only made the serious shortcomings of prohibition enforcement even more dispiriting, they helped conceal the genuine, although more modest, achievements of prohibition as a social reform. Ironically, legislative victory gutted the Anti-Saloon League as a practical political force and drained the vitality from temperance reform as a social movement.

Wheeler's unshakable faith in the effectiveness of political pressure, along with his egocentric compulsion to act as the nation's "dry boss," led the Anti-Saloon League to play politics with the Volstead Act. Wheeler arranged key features of the prohibition enforcement law so as to give the League (and himself, as the ASL's enforcement watchdog) a more direct hand in the administration of the law, even when such measures opened the Prohibition Bureau to political horse-trading and corruption. For example, political calculations were behind the assignment of prohibition enforcement to the Trea-

sury Department rather than the Justice Department. In 1919
Wheeler had argued that since the Internal Revenue Service
had enforced the liquor excise tax, "the machinery [was] already built" in Treasury for expert prohibition administration.
As Andrew Sinclair has pointed out, however, additional mo-
tives underlay League enthusiasm for this arrangement. The
overworked IRS commissioner resented the additional burden of prohibition enforcement and, upon Wheeler's informal
offer of assistance, gratefully surrendered many Prohibition
Bureau duties into the eager hands of League officials. As
long as the exhausted Internal Revenue Service was responsible for prohibition enforcement, the League had access to
power and authority.

No feature of the Volstead Act was more audacious, or
more self-defeating, than the provision that exempted Prohibition Bureau agents from civil service requirements, thus
guaranteeing that political considerations would determine
appointments to the agency empowered to enforce prohibition. Wheeler defended this arrangement because he believed
it allowed the ASL to make better use of its political influence.
Civil servants were largely immune to the pressure that the
League applied so adeptly to elected officials. Open appointments, on the other hand, allowed Wheeler to exert substantial influence over the Prohibition Bureau. After the Democratic Wilson administration gave way to Warren Harding's
Republican presidency in 1921, Wheeler used his influence
with the new president, a friend and fellow Ohioan, to install
Roy A. Haynes as head of the Prohibition Bureau. Cast out of
office was John F. Kramer, whose attempts to enforce prohibition had pleased drys, but who had the misfortune of being a
Democrat. Haynes, a little-known Ohio Republican newspaper editor prone to making grandiose claims about the successes of prohibition enforcement, appealed to Wheeler

because he was pliable. Wheeler's "endorsement was practically required for most appointments" while Haynes ran the Bureau, recalled Wheeler's secretary. Despite charges of ineffectiveness launched at Haynes, some from within the Anti-Saloon League, Wheeler staunchly stood by him until 1925 when Lincoln C. Andrews took charge of prohibition enforcement.

Wheeler also used the political patronage available in Bureau appointments to maintain a dry Congress and gain influence for himself in the Republican party. In a sense he was trapped in the electoral mentality that had gripped the ASL during its rise to prominence. He focused more on protecting the dry majority in Congress than on effectively enforcing the law. His willingness to dispense patronage in return for dry pledges kept Congress safely committed to prohibition during the 1920s, but at considerable cost to the law Wheeler sought to safeguard. What one critic called "the slimy trail of the spoils serpent" fouled efforts to make prohibition work. In 1927 a veteran prohibition official in New York complained that "three-fourths of the 2,500 dry agents are ward heelers and sycophants named by the politicians." The spoils system in the Prohibition Bureau became so powerful that not even Wheeler could prevent several objectionable appointments. In 1927, the final year of his life, he agreed to legislation that made the Prohibition Bureau independent of the Treasury Department and placed its agents under civil service. Only 40 percent of Prohibition Bureau agents passed the first civil service test under the new rule.

Wheeler's efforts to insinuate himself into the inner circle of the Republican party, partly through the use of patronage, also damaged the nonpartisan standing of the Anti-Saloon League and fomented discord within the League. Republican political domination in the 1920s, Wheeler's ardent Republican sympathies and personal ties to the Harding and Coolidge administrations, along with the rise of the wet, urban wing of the Democratic party led by New York governor Al Smith, led Wheeler into a closer alliance with the GOP than many League officials felt was suitable for a nonpartisan organization. Cannon, the most prominent ASL Democrat, was particularly offended by Wheeler's partisanship and sniped at him incessantly.

Resistance within the League to Wheeler's "personally conducted enforcement" of prohibition widened into an internal struggle for control of the organization after ailing National Superintendent Purley Baker died in 1924. Wheeler managed to replace Baker with F. Scott McBride, another weak reed whom he could control, thus disappointing Cannon and his candidate Ernest Cherrington. Wheeler's sudden death three years later prompted tributes to his dedicated service from League associates, but few lamented the passing of "Wheelerism." In a gruff response to Wheeler's legacy of partisanship, Cherrington remarked that "the most important factor in the movement against alcoholism is not the next election but the next generation." But the ASL was by then in tatters, unable to influence either American politics or American culture.

That was partly so because the enactment of national prohibition returned the advantage to politicians. Elected officials, as always, wished to eliminate the liquor issue from politics. Despite the public controversy over prohibition during the 1920s, the platforms of the national political parties remained silent on the matter. Even as disagreements between wet and dry Democrats grew increasingly boisterous, formal party pronouncements on the issue remained tightly noncommittal. "Prohibition was not a party issue in the right sense of the word, in either party," Franklin D. Roosevelt cautioned in a

1929 letter that summarized the attitude of most professional politicians. "It seems to me that we should not label anything a party principle unless it is a principle of the great majority of our party." Despite the loud squawking of wet and dry enthusiasts in the parties, in the 1920s discreet silence remained the preferred political response to prohibition.

Ratification of the 18th Amendment and passage of the Volstead Act paradoxically allowed elected officials to ignore prohibition. Most of official Washington, from President Harding on down, emphasized the moral duty of Americans to obey the law, but, as Charles Merz showed, few of them seemed anxious to draw attention to prohibition. During the first four years of prohibition, Congress passed only one additional law bearing on the matter (it prevented doctors from prescribing beer as medicine). More revealing was the modest outlay of money granted by the national government and the states to carry out the mammoth task of enforcing the dry laws.

A few thousand well-trained and active agents would have been hard-pressed to police the *legal* traffic in alcohol allowed by the Volstead Act. Production of industrial alcohol in the United States rose from 28 million gallons in 1920 to 81 million gallons five years later. Thirty denaturing plants added ingredients to the alcohol to render it unfit for beverage purposes, but strict oversight was required to prevent diversion of the alcohol before it was denatured. Similarly, near beer (that is, beer with an alcohol content of less than 0.5 percent) was legal during prohibition but could be produced only by brewing real beer and then removing the alcohol. Without tight supervision, unscrupulous brewers could easily siphon illegal beer to thirsty markets. Keeping track of liquor permits held by thousands of druggists and doctors also would occupy the efforts of prohibition enforcers.

Such tasks were onerous, but the prospect of patrolling thousands of miles of unguarded borders and coastline to prevent smuggling, or tramping through the countryside and city neighborhoods to destroy illegal stills or shut down hidden saloons, was truly daunting. The unwillingness of many Americans, especially in cities, to obey dry laws which had been passed over their protest created a market for smugglers and bootleggers. Canada's prohibition laws had been modified in the early 1920s, so Canadian distilleries and breweries furnished a supply of liquor not far from the centers of American wet resistance to prohibition. Even if most Americans submitted to the prohibition laws, a major commitment of government resources would be required to make prohibition work. American government, at all levels, failed that test.

The Prohibition Bureau received little support from other federal agencies. The Coast Guard, especially after new ships and men were added in 1924, helped interdict seaborne smuggling. On land, customs agents and, to a lesser extent, immigration officers also seized smuggled liquor. Yet these efforts to seal the borders stopped only about 5 percent of the liquor smuggled into the United States in 1925, according to Prohibition Bureau head Lincoln Andrews. Neither the Coast Guard nor the Customs Service had the resources to go beyond piecemeal operations. Interagency rivalries undercut efforts to coordinate intelligence and improve overall enforcement. At the federal level, the Prohibition Bureau had to enforce prohibition on its own.

For prohibition to be effective, Prohibition Bureau commissioner Kramer had stressed at the outset, Congress needed to allocate sufficient funds to attract a large force of agents at salaries high enough to minimize the dangers of bribery and corruption. For their part, the states had to commit similar resources to guarantee the concurrent enforcement of the law.

Instead, from 1921 to 1926 congressional appropriations for the Prohibition Bureau hovered between $6 million and $10 million. That supported the employment of about 3,060 agents yearly, with salaries ranging from $1,200 to under $2,300. The presence of some highly effective officers (the ability of agents Izzy Einstein and Moe Smith to penetrate bootlegging operations through the ingenious use of disguise made them national celebrities) could not offset the poor quality and low morale of many underpaid Prohibition Bureau field agents. During the first six years of prohibition, one of every twelve Bureau agents was fired for taking bribes, issuing illegal permits, conspiring to sell illegal liquor, or other corrupt acts. In one federal courthouse during one month in 1925, fifty-eight policemen and prohibition agents were convicted of conspiring to break the prohibition laws. Weakened by patronage, infested with corruption, hampered by the lack of resources, and disrupted by frequent administrative shakeups and transfer of personnel, the Prohibition Bureau proved itself unfit as an effective enforcement agency.

In the states the situation was even worse. With the exception of Maryland, whose governor, Albert Ritchie, became a leader of the resistance to national prohibition, all the states enacted "baby Volstead" laws in the early 1920s to accompany the national prohibition statute. Some state laws were even harsher than the Volstead Act, outlawing the personal possession of liquor and giving local authorities greater power to search out and seize illegal alcohol. But little money was spent to back up these laws. By 1923 the states contributed less than $550,000 to enforce prohibition; the total in 1927 was about $690,000. In the latter year twenty-eight states with enforcement laws allocated no funds at all to enforce prohibition. Observers noted that state expenditures for prohibition totaled only one-fourth of the amount states spent to maintain parks

and monuments and one-eighth of the funds expended to enforce fish and game laws. Some states turned away from even
symbolic compliance with prohibition. New York repealed its
enforcement act in 1923, followed over the next six years by
Massachusetts, Montana, and Wisconsin. The doctrine of concurrent state and national prohibition laws, which the Anti-
Saloon League had used to great effect in the prohibition
drive, now backfired disastrously on the drys.

Prohibition enforcement in the cities was still more slack.
Police officers who attempted to enforce the national prohibition laws in 1921 were actually reprimanded by the San Francisco Board of Supervisors. Honest efforts to enforce the law
in Philadelphia and Chicago produced thousands of arrests
but few convictions, as juries turned their neighbors loose
until the crusading spirit among prosecutors and city officials
waned. Smedley D. Butler, a Marine general brought in to dry
up Philadelphia, announced in frustration that "the path of
law enforcement has been blocked by powerful influences, by
legal machinery that should have been an aid, and by the invo-
cation of technicalities." After two years of exhausting effort,
Chicago mayor William Dever expressed the desire "to pass
the burden of [prohibition enforcement] on to somebody else,
or else from the aid of constructive legislation to be relieved of
its annoyance."

The futility of enforcing prohibition laws in urban court-
rooms became apparent in 1928 when a San Francisco jury in
a liquor case came under indictment for drinking the evidence. Everywhere overburdened courts collapsed under the
weight of cases generated by prohibition. Without state or federal funds to hire more clerks and judges to handle rampant
liquor-law violations, courts by 1925 resorted to the expedient
of "bargain days" to clear the dockets. On bargain days, defen-
dants who waived jury trials and pleaded guilty to violating

prohibition laws received small fines rather than prison sentences. Without adequate support from Washington or state capitals, prohibition enforcement quickly broke down.

Most American political leaders were content with meager enforcement. It is hard to dispute Merz's biting judgment that "the real mission of the [Prohibition] Bureau was not to enforce the law effectively . . . but to go through the motions of enough enforcement to give Congress a clean bill of health." Small appropriations for prohibition enforcement also fit the cost-cutting policies and retreat from government activism that marked the 1920s Republican ascendancy. Despite verbal support for prohibition from Harding (who, in deference to the spirit of the law, curtailed his own drinking before he died in 1923) and his successor Calvin Coolidge, neither president asked for greater enforcement measures. Congress actually appropriated slightly more money for prohibition enforcement than either the Harding or Coolidge administrations requested.

For its own reasons, the Anti-Saloon League went along with the fiction that prohibition enforcement could be accomplished with minimal expenditures. In response to an alarming claim that real enforcement required upwards of $50 million annually, Wayne Wheeler declared in 1920 that a $5 million budget would do the job. Wheeler and his colleagues wanted to present prohibition as a workable, effective social policy, not an unpopular directive that could be enforced only with an army of government agents and massive expenditures. As prohibition faltered, the League demanded better enforcement, but it failed to sway officeholders. Most Americans, it seemed, were also content with strict laws and lax enforcement. After 1920 the mass movement that had sustained the League in its campaign for prohibition eroded.

The ASL had made itself the indispensable agent of dry activism by turning the focus of alcohol reform away from the soul of the drinker to the machinery of the liquor industry. Once achieved, prohibition dismantled the liquor industry; many erstwhile supporters of the League, thinking their work done, stopped contributing money and ceased writing letters to officeholders. Financial support for the League dropped so sharply that in 1921 the outspoken William Anderson bluntly announced that "the Anti-Saloon League is afflicted with dry rot." Money troubles led Anderson, who had directed the New York ASL with characteristic aggressiveness since 1914, to juggle League books to cover expenses. The resulting irregularities, pounced upon by Anderson's many political foes, resulted in a forgery conviction for Anderson in 1924 and a short but humiliating prison term which deeply embarrassed the League. More damaging was an investigation by the Federal Council of Churches, made public in 1925, that condemned the League's political strategy for prohibition enforcement. Without the firm support of organized Protestantism, the League could not pressure Congress to take sterner action to enforce the law.

Legislative success undercut prohibition reform in one additional, ironic fashion. For thirty years the ASL had blamed the liquor traffic for poverty, crime, disease, and corrupt politics. Once the drink industry was overturned, prohibition itself was blamed for the persistence of social evils. "In wet territory, the sight of a drunken man in the gutter brings the comment: 'See what the liquor traffic has done!'" observed Daniel M. Gandier, the insightful leader of the California ASL. "In prohibition United States a drunken man will bring the comment 'See what prohibition has done!'" This reversal of moral culpability exaggerated the actual (and serious) abuses associated with prohibition and ignored the extent to which prohibition changed the drinking culture of Americans.

Although most historians stress the obvious failures of prohibition, some assess it more positively. Twenty years ago Norman Clark advanced the novel argument that prohibition "was at least *partially successful.*" More recently John C. Burnham has gone further, asserting that "contrary to myth, Prohibition was substantially successful." If prohibition is viewed as the product of a social reform movement intent on destroying saloons and the culture of male drinking they sheltered, it did indeed achieve some of its goals. Prohibition wiped out what Clark calls the "old-time" saloon that was owned by breweries and catered to an exclusively male clientele. The custom of treating, which was central to the male culture of saloons, disappeared amid the high prices and clandestine circumstances of prohibition-era speakeasies, as the illegal drinking resorts of the dry years came to be called. The nightclubs, cafés, bars, and restaurants in which Americans drank after prohibition were not simply saloons with new names but elements of a new culture of entertainment which differed from the saloon-centered nineteenth-century world of drinking.

More immediately, prohibition curtailed, at least temporarily, the working-class drinking that had worried progressive observers at the turn of the century. Illegal liquor, though available in cities, was too expensive for most working-class incomes. In a 1928 study, the economist Irving Fisher estimated that the cost of a quart of beer had increased 600 percent since 1916, the price of gin had gone up 520 percent, and whiskey cost 150 percent more. Clark reported that a whiskey highball cost fifteen cents in 1919 Chicago but rose to seventy-five cents after the Volstead Act. Many working-class drinkers were simply priced out of the market.

Some evidence indicates that the context of drinking and

the behavior it produced also changed under prohibition. A coal company president told congressional investigators that "there is some moonshine liquor, some home-brew, and some bootleg, but the old days of the pay-day whoopee are gone. What drinking there is, is under cover, the practice of drinking up a whole month's pay, and challenging the world to mortal combat has passed." In other words, some of the alarming public manifestations of the culture of male drinking had faded.

Most significant was the decline in overall drinking that prohibition initiated. Estimates put the average annual consumption of absolute alcohol by Americans of drinking age (fifteen years and above) at 2.56 gallons between 1911 and 1915, just before state prohibition and federal laws began effectively to dry up the country. Precise measurements of alcohol consumption during national prohibition are impossible, but in 1934, after prohibition had ended, alcohol consumption had fallen to 0.97 gallons. It remained below the 1911–1915 average for fifty years. Not until 1970 did Americans again drink as much as 2.5 gallons of absolute alcohol. Prohibition, in short, introduced a half-century of temperate drinking in America.

But advocates of prohibition had made larger claims for their reform. They did not intend to reduce drinking in America but to eliminate alcohol as a problem in American life. They promised to enforce the law rigorously and make prohibition the centerpiece of a prosperous, law-abiding, and unified American nation. By those standards, prohibition failed disastrously. Still, few Americans in the mid-1920s envisioned the repeal of constitutional prohibition, just its gradual decay as enforced social policy. Significant cultural shifts and the Great Depression—a devastating economic disaster whose impact was similar to the wartime emergency that hastened the adoption of prohibition—led to its unanticipated over-throw, even as Herbert Hoover became the first American president to attempt real enforcement of the law.

8

The Shock of Repeal

BY THE MID-1920s the weaknesses of national prohibition were well known. Most Americans nevertheless believed that prohibition, set into the granite of the United States Constitution, had become a permanent fixture in the nation's public life. Even as vociferous a wet as Clarence Darrow, the famed attorney and civil libertarian, acknowledged the seeming unassailability of prohibition. "Even to modify the Volstead Act would require a political revolution," he glumly conceded in 1924. "To repeal the Eighteenth Amendment is well-nigh inconceivable."

In 1929 Herbert Hoover became the first president during prohibition to commit himself to more stringent enforcement of the law. Just before he took office, Congress raised the maximum punishment for first-time violators of the Volstead Act to five years in prison and $10,000 in fines. Critics complained that the five federal penitentiaries were already overcrowded with liquor-law violators. In response, Hoover authorized the construction of six additional federal prisons, including Alcatraz in San Francisco Bay; by 1930 more than one-third of the 12,332 federal inmates were Volstead Act offenders. Also in 1930, the Prohibition Bureau was finally transferred to the Justice Department, with the expectation that it would function with greater efficiency. Nearly a decade after its adoption as the law of the land, it appeared that prohibition might actually be put to the test. Yet by the end of 1933 the 18th Amendment had been repealed, and national prohibition, once the shining goal of reform aspirations, slipped into popular memory as a laughable and embarrassing episode in misdirected zeal. A generation later the historian Richard Hofstadter dismissed it as a "pseudo-reform" perpetrated on the nation by the cranky remnants of the rural, evangelical culture of the nineteenth century.

The popular repudiation of prohibition, which Hofstadter's biting judgment accurately reflected, was the product of social, cultural, political, and economic developments that between 1926 and 1933 came together with astonishing force. They did not significantly alter ethnic and working-class opposition to the dry laws, which remained relatively constant throughout the 1920s. Instead, the depth of the repudiation stemmed from the erosion of middle-class support for prohibition. Americans who had demanded the suppression of the saloon at the turn of the century were troubled by the crime, corruption, and governmental incompetence that accompanied prohibition. Unlike the Progressive Era, when the argument against prohibition was left to representatives of the despised liquor trades or marginalized immigrant or working-class associations, by the late 1920s business leaders, professionals, and women's groups raised their voices in opposition to prohibition, primarily through the Association Against the Prohibition Amendment (AAPA) and the Women's Organization for National Prohibition Reform (WONPR).

The cultural significance of drinking had also shifted by the late 1920s, realigning middle-class attitudes toward prohibition. Despite the bureaucratic innovations of the Anti-Saloon League, a constellation of values formed in the Victorian

Era—a culture of duty and denial, of faith in God and progress, that sought to protect the family and impose order on society—deeply influenced dry sentiment into the twentieth century. The pervasively secular consumer culture of the 1920s, with its emphasis on youth, self-fulfillment, and entertainment, overwhelmed the older middle-class culture that had celebrated prohibition as a necessary reform. Whereas saloons had offended middle-class sensibilities before prohibition, prohibition-era speakeasies furnished enjoyment and a hint of illegal adventure to the self-indulgent new middle class of the 1920s.

Even middle-class women's support for prohibition, a central article of faith in the dry movement, fractured in the 1920s. Observers on both sides of the liquor debate at the turn of the century had anticipated that women, once enfranchised, would form a powerful bloc of dry voters. But after women gained the vote in 1920, they demonstrated not unity of outlook but rather a variety of political opinions on prohibition as well as other public issues. The breakdown of traditional saloon culture in fact opened the way for women's participation in the new atmosphere of public drinking taking shape in speakeasies. When the repeal movement gained momentum after 1929, American women did not flock to the defense of prohibition.

Alterations in middle-class culture help explain the extent of prohibition's vulnerability by the end of the twenties, but the startling suddenness of repeal was the result of political and economic events. After years of evasion by both Democrats and Republicans, the liquor issue crept back into national politics. Spurred by the 1928 presidential candidacy of Al Smith, a prominent opponent of the Volstead Act, Herbert Hoover's growing identification with prohibition after 1929, and intense internal debates in both parties, prohibition became an issue in the 1932 presidential election. The Democratic party forced its cautious candidate, Franklin D. Roosevelt, to embrace repeal while Hoover dragged a reluctant GOP into open support for the continuation of what Hoover had once described as "a great social and economic experiment"— this despite the critical assessment of prohibition issued in 1931 by Hoover's own special investigative body, the National Commission on Law Observance and Enforcement, popularly known as the Wickersham Commission.

Overshadowing Hoover's efforts to defend prohibition, and casting a pall on his hopes for reelection in 1932, was the enormous specter of the Great Depression. As the national economy crashed down around them, Americans came to view Hoover with disdain. The president's assurances of a quick return to prosperity and his futile appeal for voluntary cooperation to reverse the collapse of the banking system and industry generated a wave of popular resentment. In light of Hoover's inability to face the facts of economic disaster, his continued insistence on the viability of prohibition appeared foolish and trivial. On the other hand, assurances from wets that repeal of prohibition would restore jobs and tax dollars offered hope at a moment of desperate scarcity. Tangled in the wreckage of Hoover's reputation, and taking on the aspect of an unnecessary burden in a time of national emergency, prohibition was jettisoned in 1933 with unusual speed and few second thoughts.

From its origins in the nineteenth century, temperance reform had developed as a forward-looking, optimistic social movement. Its proponents had been modernizers, those who looked forward to social, economic, and moral improvement. That image became badly tarnished in the 1920s as prohibition came to be labeled the creaky obsession of puritanical moralists, rural busybodies, and religious bigots. One of the most damaging blows to the reform image of prohibition was the dry enthusiasm exhibited by the hooded knights of the resurgent Ku Klux Klan. The Klan of the 1920s took its name from the terrorist band of Southern night riders that intimidated black voters and federal officials during Reconstruction; but the new KKK, founded in Georgia in 1915, appealed to a wider constituency of native-born white Protestants. Cleverly marketed (by an Atlanta public relations firm which had done work for the Anti-Saloon League) to take advantage of the postwar boom in fraternal associations, and using the popularity of D. W. Griffith's heroic portrayal of the original Klan in the film *The Birth of a Nation* as a recruiting tool, the new Klan attracted from three to six million members in all sections of the country between 1920 and 1925, including women in a Klan auxiliary. During that period the revived Klan became a political force in many communities and briefly controlled state politics in Oregon, Colorado, and Indiana.

The 1920s Klan expressed an outlook variously described by Klan historians as "white Protestant nationalism" or "reactionary populism." This viewpoint asserted white Protestant superiority over blacks, Catholics, Jews, and immigrants but also eyed social and economic elites with suspicion. It demanded an end to radicalism, loose morality, law-breaking, and political corruption. Klansmen shined flashlights into the startled eyes of young couples parked in lovers' lanes, threatened adulterers and wife beaters with vigilante justice, and, most of all, insisted that prohibition laws be respected. Leonard Moore, one of the leading historians of the Klan, asserts that "support for Prohibition represented the single most important bond between Klansmen throughout the nation." No other issue so revealed the dangerous decline of law and order at the local level. So Klansmen became active advocates of prohibition enforcement, working through mainstream politics in states such as Indiana, Colorado, Oregon, and New York, but adding touches of vigilante violence in the South and especially the Southwest. There the alacrity with which Klansmen applied "a horsewhip or a razorstrop to suspected bootleggers" attracted national criticism.

Fearing what Wayne Wheeler called the "detrimental" consequences of a perceived link between the Anti-Saloon League and the Klan, the League sought to distance itself from the Invisible Empire. At the local level, however, the Klan and the ASL often were closely associated. As early as 1919, Atlanta Klansmen and ASL members took part in a torchlit march to celebrate the onset of prohibition. A former League president in Georgia was a prominent Klan sympathizer. The head of the Indiana ASL, Edward Schumaker, became a political and legislative ally of the powerful Indiana Klan. Schumaker further embarrassed the League in a dispute with the state attorney general that ended with a jail term for the controversial League official. The outspoken William Anderson defended the Klan's role in New York politics and emerged from his prison term in the mid-twenties as a fierce anti-Catholic. Meanwhile the chief League official in Buffalo actually joined the KKK. Anxious to avoid the taint of bigotry and vigilante action, the League nevertheless found itself and the cause of prohibition yoked to the Klan's disturbing image.

Dry political maneuvers furthered the impression that prohibitionists shared the intolerant outlook of the Klan, especially its anti-Catholicism. The dry wing of the Democratic party prevented the passage of a platform statement denouncing the KKK during its raucous 1924 party convention. Four years later Bishop James Cannon, the most prominent ASL Democrat, rebelled against the nomination of Al Smith for president and implored Southern Democrats to cross party lines to elect Herbert Hoover. Cannon insisted that his bitter opposition to Smith stemmed from the New Yorker's wet convictions, but during the campaign Cannon wrote a slanderous advertisement entitled "Is Southern Protestantism More Intolerant Than Romanism?," pilloried Democratic National Committee chairman John J. Raskob as "this wet Roman Catholic Knight of Columbus and chamberlain of the Pope of Rome," and privately characterized Smith as an example of "the intolerant, bigoted type, characteristic of the Irish Roman Catholic hierarchy of New York City." Few observers failed to miss the symmetry of views between Cannon and the cloaked representatives of the Ku Klux Klan. As one Virginia reporter noted with matter-of-fact clarity, "the dry and klan forces" were united in the anti-Smith movement.

Even the collapse of the KKK as a political force amid scandal and legislative disappointment seemed to mirror the troubles that beset dry leaders in the 1920s. The often sincere hope among Klan members that the political influence of the Invisible Empire would purify government crumbled at mid-decade. Reports of cronyism, financial misdeeds, and moral outrages—topped by the sensational 1925 revelation that the flamboyant Indiana Klansman D. C. Stephenson had drugged, chewed on, and raped a woman, then hid her in his mansion after she took an ultimately fatal dose of poison—brought down powerful Klan leaders and their political allies. Membership in the Klan plummeted thereafter, amid comments that public moralists appeared to be personal liars and miscreants.

Similar judgments were applied to prohibitionists after the jailing of Anderson and the prosecution of Schumaker and other League officials. *The Nation* remarked in 1926 on "the Anti-Saloon League's lost virtue." In early 1927, following the deaths of several dozen holiday revelers from drinking bootleg liquor contaminated with wood alcohol, the press denounced the League as a ghoulish band of poisoners because Wayne Wheeler defended the use of the toxic substance as a denaturant. Then, in 1930, Cannon himself was brought low by charges of hoarding flour during World War I, speculating in stocks, misappropriating funds during the 1928 campaign, and committing adultery with his secretary. Although Cannon was never convicted of wrongdoing, the moral authority by which the ASL hoped to retain middle-class enthusiasm for prohibition shriveled. Neither the Klan nor the ASL, the two most prominent defenders of prohibition by 1925, seemed worthy of respectable support.

If the violent images evoked by the hooded figures of the Ku Klux Klan undermined prohibition, violence of another sort accelerated popular frustration with the dry laws. Before the adoption of national prohibition, organized criminal enterprise in the United States was considered part of the seamy underside of saloon culture. As the numerous vice commissions that formed in Progressive Era cities discovered, an underworld of criminality, mainly gambling and prostitution, operated on the shadowy margins of saloon life. Prohibition offered young, energetic lieutenants within existing crime organizations opportunities to branch out into the profitable commerce in illegal liquor. Most of the leading criminal bootleggers, according to the historian Humbert Nelli, were ambitious Italian, Polish, or Jewish men in their twenties and early thirties whose youth and immigrant origins had restricted their rise within traditional criminal organizations. "Everybody calls me a racketeer," complained Al Capone of Chicago, the most notorious of the gangland bootleggers by his mid-twenties. "I call myself a businessman." For such men, supplying liquor to the estimated 219,000 speakeasies in prohibition America became a formula for social mobility.

Corruption and violence accompanied the rise of criminal bootlegging gangs. Gangsters hijacked cargoes of illegal liquor from their competitors, bribed police and public officials, and, most sensationally, engaged in bloody territorial battles. In Chicago alone between 1920 and 1930, almost 550 criminals died at the hands of their rivals; the police killed a few hundred more. Gang warfare in New York killed more than a thousand people. Such highly visible violence created public fears of a "prohibition crime wave." Statisticians cautioned that the murder rate, although climbing steadily since 1900, had made its biggest jump well before the coming of prohibition. Nevertheless a burst of violence in Chicago between 1926 and 1929, which included the murder of an assistant state's attorney, brutal criminal interference in elections, and the machine-gunning of seven rival bootleggers by Capone's men in the famous St. Valentine's Day Massacre, reinforced the popular linkage of prohibition with unbridled criminality. The celebrity status of gangland figures, magnified by the appearance in the early 1930s of gangster films featuring charismatic stars such as James Cagney and Edward G. Robinson as appealing criminal entrepreneurs, as well as the commonplace violation of the Volstead Act, furthered the impression that prohibition had brought a dangerous quality of lawlessness to American society.

Opponents of prohibition also condemned the violence and incompetence with which the law was enforced. Critics claimed that gunplay between federal officers and smugglers resulted in more than a thousand deaths. (The government acknowledged 286 killings, including agents and civilians.) Incidents in which the undisciplined fire of Prohibition Bureau agents hurt or killed innocent bystanders, including several children and a United States senator, were widely publicized by the Association Against the Prohibition Amendment, which in 1929 gathered them together in a pamphlet entitled *Reforming America with a Shotgun*.

Other observers complained that dry lawmen abused their authority. After prohibition agents entered the lakeside property of Henry Joy, wealthy president of the Packard Motor Company, to shoot at smugglers and seize the modest alcoholic stock of his watchman, the businessman protested that "the people live in fear of unlawful search of their homes and their motor cars as they travel, and unlawful shootings and killings by the officers of the Treasury Department." By the late 1920s many prominent citizens had come to the conclusion that prohibition fostered a contempt for law and order both among those who defied the law and those entrusted to enforce it.

Changing social mores further corroded respect for prohibition among the middle class. "It is safe to say that a significant change has taken place in the social attitude toward drinking," concluded the Wickersham Commission in 1931 after extensive investigation into the drinking habits of Americans. Although Americans as a whole were drinking less during prohibition, the context of drinking, especially middle-class drinking, had undergone a transformation since prohibition shut down the old-time saloon. An intersection of powerful social forces—an assertive youth movement, new patterns of sexual dynamics, and demands for leisure-time amusements spurred by an expanding consumer economy—broke down the saloon culture of male drinking and replaced it with a culture of youthful, recreational drinking which emphasized social contact between men and women.

One need not accept overdrawn portraits of a hedonistic Jazz Age to recognize the shift in values and behavior from Victorian patterns to the recognizably modern emphasis on entertainment and personal fulfillment that became apparent during the 1920s. Social life was recast for working-class and middle-class Americans alike by automobiles, radio, and the movies. Before World War I, Roy Rosenzweig reports, movies began to compete with saloons as centers of working-class leisure. In the 1920s movies and public drinking became middle-class amusements, especially among the young. On college campuses, polls revealed, two of three students drank alcoholic beverages during prohibition. For some, carrying hip flasks and engaging in the occasional display of public drunkenness reflected the "smart," cosmopolitan outlook one found in the irreverent films of the period. More important was the fact, revealed by the historian Paula Fass, that by the mid-twenties college men and women drank together.

As the historian Mary Murphy has noted, "Drinking in the late nineteenth and early twentieth centuries was one of the most gender-segregated activities in the United States." Men drank in saloons; women, if they drank, did so at home. Prohibition helped alter that arrangement. Murphy found that in Butte, Montana, the closing of saloons opened up opportunities for women to enter "spaces that had once been reserved exclusively for men." Women—young and old, working class and middle class—manufactured and sold bootleg liquor. More remarkably, women in groups and in the company of young men were welcomed in the liquor-serving restaurants and nightclubs that had replaced the saloons.

From New York to Butte, the dismantling of the saloon-based drinking environment introduced new possibilities for social interaction in the clandestine drinking establishments that took their place. In some cities, interracial contact became far more common in speakeasies than had been the case in saloons. In New York, the historian George Chauncey reports, the city's gay subculture flourished in the shifting public space of prohibition nightclubs. Most common, however, was the development of what Murphy calls "a new heterosocial nightlife." Speakeasies as well as movie theaters and restaurants catered to the new custom of dating, defined by Fass as a "ritual of sexual interaction" less binding than courting, its nineteenth-century predecessor. In the 1920s drinking and dating were meant to be entertaining and experimental. In that context, elders often preached control rather than abstinence. In a 1931 magazine article, one woman expressed the wish that her grandsons "know the difference between drinking like gentlemen and lapping it up like puppies." From such experiences was the legend born that drinking actually increased during prohibition. In reality, it was middle-class exposure to drinking that grew during the dry years.

By the late 1920s middle-class complaints that prohibition fostered crime, subverted respect for laws and government, and threatened society rather than purified it had grown powerful enough to sustain a movement among business and professional people against the 18th Amendment. Between 1928 and 1930, for example, opposition to prohibition among lawyers grew more pronounced. The bar associations of eight cities and three states called for an end to federal liquor controls. In 1929 a coalition of respected attorneys organized the Voluntary Committee of Lawyers to combat national prohibition. After a quiet campaign by the VCL, an American Bar Association referendum in 1930 produced a two-to-one ratio in favor of repeal.

Two other significant organizations opposed to prohibition formed in 1929. One of them, a young men's association called the Crusaders (inspired, it was later claimed, by anger following the St. Valentine's Day Massacre), ultimately attracted nearly one million members but produced few tangible results. The other, the Women's Organization for National Prohibition Reform, was both politically influential and symbolically important. Organized by Pauline Sabin, a socially prominent figure who was also influential in the Republican party, the WONPR offered a firm rebuttal to the claim that all American women stood behind national prohibition. Privately convinced that prohibition violated constitutional liberties and produced in the young "a total lack of respect for the Constitution and for the law," Sabin took dramatic public action after hearing WCTU president Ella Boole claim in 1928 to speak for the women of America.

Many of the leaders of the WONPR (including Sabin) were married to prominent, wealthy advocates of the anti-prohibition cause, sparking dry accusations that the WONPR was simply a glamorous front organization for male-dominated repeal groups. In the bitter yet picturesque language of onetime reformer Fletcher Dobyns, cynical wets, "in true Russian fashion, . . . ordered their wives and daughters into the trenches" to bring down prohibition. But research by David Kyvig, Kenneth Rose, and Caryn Neumann has established that the WONPR maintained an independent and effective political presence and attracted the allegiance of women from all social classes. By 1933 the WONPR, which did not demand dues from its supporters, claimed 1.5 million members. Although Kyvig, the chief authority on repeal organizations, cannot verify that figure, he concludes that the WONPR was still "by far the largest antiprohibition association."

The most influential group in the repeal coalition was the oldest, the Association Against the Prohibition Amendment. The AAPA shaped popular anti-prohibition sentiment into effective action, worked closely with the other major repeal groups, and orchestrated the political campaign that ended national prohibition. Founded in 1918 by William Stayton, a former naval officer, to resist the adoption of the 18th Amendment, the AAPA grew into a significant force in the mid-1920s by attracting the support of prominent business leaders, most notably Pierre, Irénée, and Lammot du Pont of the giant chemical firm, and John J. Raskob, Pierre du Pont's associate at Du Pont and General Motors. Also involved were political figures such as James Wadsworth, former Republican senator from New York, and Maryland Democrat William Cabell Bruce. Although the AAPA expressed dismay at the reports of increased crime, violence, corruption, and excessive drinking associated with prohibition, Kyvig has shown that the core of its opposition to national prohibition was a conservative political conviction that the dry laws represented an unwarranted intrusion of national government into local and private affairs.

Even as the dry movement lost its momentum as a forward-looking reform, the leading anti-prohibition body also anchored its argument in the past, drawing its suspicion of government impingements on individual liberty and state's rights from the political traditions of Jefferson and Jackson. "The Prohibition Amendment is not merely an *impairment* of the principle of self-government of the States," explained one AAPA convert, "it constitutes an absolute abandonment of that principle." Stayton and other AAPA figures used the same ground to oppose the adoption of federal standards to regulate child labor. AAPA officials pointed to a series of legal decisions and laws tied to prohibition enforcement to fortify their contention that national prohibition had upended constitutional protections. A 1920 Supreme Court decision, *Hawke v. Smith*, upheld the Ohio legislature's ratification of the 18th Amendment, even though a popular referendum subsequently rejected ratification. Two years later the Supreme Court ruled in *United States v. Lanza* that violators of prohibition laws could be prosecuted by both federal and state courts for the same infraction. The first decision, AAPA publicists argued, silenced popular democracy; the second tore down the constitutional ban on double jeopardy. When Congress increased the penalties for first-time Volstead Act violators with the Jones Act in 1929, the AAPA argued that the law vindictively punished small fry with the same severity it showed to major bootleggers.

Firm in its conviction that major constitutional questions were at stake, the AAPA moved away from early attempts to modify the Volstead Act and decided in 1928 to agitate for outright repeal of the 18th Amendment. Although the association carried fewer members than other anti-prohibition groups, it used its substantial financial resources to influence public opinion. AAPA researchers investigated the social, political, and economic costs of prohibition in a series of mass-produced pamphlets. Other AAPA publications explored alternative forms of liquor control practiced in other nations. The analytical tone and wealth of detail in the reports made them newsworthy as the national debate over prohibition intensified. AAPA publicists fed them to newspapers and magazines where they reached a nationwide audience. Along the way the AAPA added members, growing to about 150,000 in 1930 and cresting at 550,000 two years later.

Through the influence of the AAPA, repeal sentiment also made inroads into the party system. New York governor Al Smith, who had signed the repeal of the Empire State's prohibition enforcement act in 1923, had been denied the 1924 Democratic presidential nomination by the party's rural, dry wing and its old hero William Jennings Bryan. In 1928 Bryan was three years dead, and the charismatic Smith, a hero to urban, ethnic Democrats, received the party's nomination. Cautious as ever on the liquor question, the Democratic platform committed the party to enforcement of the 18th Amendment. Smith, however, made no secret of his belief that prohibition was a decision for state and local authorities, not the federal government. Doomed by his Catholicism and background in urban machine politics to failure in the 1928 election (five solidly Democratic Southern states voted for Hoover against Smith), Smith nevertheless began to tilt the Democratic party to the wet side of the prohibition debate, especially by appointing John J. Raskob, a former Republican, as chairman of the Democratic National Committee. Raskob, a member of the AAPA's governing board, worked with almost single-minded energy over the next four years to convert Democrats to an official endorsement of prohibition repeal.

The final drama of the prohibition decade was also taking shape in the Republican party. Urged on by its dry enthusiasts, the GOP platform moved beyond its usual vague homage to law and order and instead promised "vigorous enforcement" of prohibition. The Republican nominee, Herbert Hoover, had been somewhat circumspect on the subject of prohibition, at one point calling the dry reform "a moral failure and an economic success." Yet Hoover believed in the rule of law and displayed the progressive confidence in the public spirit. He therefore announced his opposition to repeal and promised to give prohibition a fair and complete trial. His position was enough to drive some prominent AAPA Republicans to support Smith. The liquor issue, in a modest way, had once again begun to reshuffle American political allegiances.

If Hoover had lost the 1928 election, which he won by more than six million votes, he would be a less prominent but more fondly remembered historical personality. As a noted engineer, a highly praised architect of American food aid to Europe after World War I, and a talented cabinet member standing above the general mediocrity and corruption of the Harding and Coolidge administrations, Hoover had forged a brilliant record of public service. The Great Depression destroyed it all. Beginning with the stock market crash of 1929 and followed by the collapse of the banking industry, the evaporation of investment, and the closing of factories and shops, the depression turned millions of Americans out of work, left farms glutted with crops that could not be sold, and provoked a bewildered, sullen population to glare angrily at their president. Hoover had urged bankers and industrialists to cooperate voluntarily to save their enterprises. When that failed, the president was slow to commit federal resources to relieve suffering. He retreated into the White House, met infrequently with the press, issued hopeful predictions that the ailing economy would right itself, and in 1932 sent the army to disperse an encampment in Washington of disgruntled World War I veterans who wanted their bonuses. Hoover had become the resented symbol of complacency and inaction in the face of disaster. "People were starving because of Herbert Hoover," insisted the aunt of young Russell Baker. "My Mother was out of work because of Herbert Hoover. Men were killing themselves because of Herbert Hoover, and their fatherless children were being packed away into orphanages . . . because of Herbert Hoover." Rarely had a public reputation unraveled so swiftly and completely.

The depression made Hoover's resolution to enforce prohibition seem desperately misplaced. Adding significantly to that impression in 1931 were the conclusions of the Wickersham Commission. Upon taking office in 1929, Hoover had named eleven respected public figures, known as moderates on the subject of prohibition, to investigate the workings of the 18th Amendment as well as crime generally in the United States. The commission produced what is still the most exhaustive examination of prohibition ever undertaken, with devastating results for Hoover and the drys. The report documented the utter disorganization and inadequacy of prohibition enforcement and the widespread defiance of the law. Although the report concluded by opposing repeal of prohibition or modification of the Volstead Act to allow the sale of beer and light wines, the individual statements appended to the conclusion were far more critical of the dry status quo. Only one commissioner was steadfast in his support for the continuation of national prohibition. Most of the others supported modification of the dry laws, with a government-regulated liquor monopoly patterned after the Swedish system attracting the majority of enthusiasm. Two commissioners called for outright repeal of the 18th Amendment.

Hoover shook off the contradictions between the summary conclusions and the personal statements of the commissioners and declared that the report supported his own policy of more efficient enforcement. To most Americans, however, the Wickersham Commission report offered definitive evidence of prohibition's failure and Hoover's folly in pursuing the enforcement of a repudiated policy. Unhappily for Republicans, the GOP now carried a double burden as the party of depression *and* prohibition.

As the depression deepened, repeal sentiment gained momentum. AAPA publications began to stress the tax savings that would result from the end of prohibition and the return of federal levies on liquor. A national poll conducted by the *Literary Digest* in 1930 recorded 30.5 percent of its participants in favor of prohibition, 29 percent urging the legalization of wine and beer, and more than 40 percent backing outright repeal. In the same year Republican party platforms in five states and Democratic party platforms in fourteen states called for repeal. Both the American Legion and the Veterans of Foreign Wars endorsed repeal in 1931, while the American Federation of Labor began to move beyond its demand to amend the Volstead Act and explore the possibility of repeal.

In 1932 the major repeal organizations, led by the AAPA, formed the United Repeal Council to help with the final push in the coming election.

Republicans in 1932 could not disentangle themselves from Hoover's ties to prohibition. Although Hoover himself came to realize that alterations in national prohibition were advisable, at the party's convention he refused to entertain the repeal initiatives of wet Republicans. Instead the party platform allowed for the possibility of a constitutional amendment open to popular ratification that would allow some autonomy on the part of the states while retaining federal control of prohibition. This last, confusing straddle on prohibition completed, the GOP forlornly prepared to go down to defeat, chained to its stubborn, taciturn leader.

Among Democrats the matter of repeal became part of an intricate struggle for control of the party before the 1932 convention. Following the 1928 election, Raskob used his position as party chairman to build an organization committed to the repeal of prohibition but also dedicated to the conservative, business-oriented, limited-government philosophy of the AAPA. The chief opponent of Raskob and the conservative Democratic coalition was New York governor Franklin D. Roosevelt, an adherent of the party's liberal, activist wing. Although Roosevelt had come out for repeal in 1930, that was in the context of New York state politics. As a cautious politician, FDR resisted efforts to commit the party and its candidate to repeal until public opinion overwhelmingly demanded it.

By the time of the 1932 convention, the party's prohibition plank became the centerpiece of a complex power struggle that pitted Roosevelt against Raskob, Al Smith, and the party conservatives. The conservatives hoped to use FDR's hesitancy to embrace repeal as a device to deny him the nomination. Once Roosevelt determined the depth of party support for repeal at the convention, however, he accepted the repeal plank, thereby disarming the conservatives and assuring his nomination for president. As Roosevelt cheerily declared his support for swift passage of a constitutional amendment to end national prohibition, Raskob and the AAPA conservatives must have realized that in winning the prohibition fight, they had lost their war for the Democratic party. By 1934 the remnants of the AAPA reorganized as the American Liberty League to wage a lonely and unpopular resistance to Roosevelt and the New Deal. To the very end, the liquor issue confounded those politicians who tried to control it.

Barriers to the repeal of the 18th Amendment fell away in the 1932 election. Roosevelt beat Hoover by more than seven million votes, a huge Democratic majority swept into Congress, and nine states voted to repeal their own prohibition enforcement laws. Before the new administration took office, Congress passed a repeal amendment specifying that special state conventions, not sitting legislatures, ratify the amendment, thus assuring popular control of the repeal process. The Voluntary Committee of Lawyers stepped forward with a formula for electing convention delegates that was immediately adopted by the states. One month after Roosevelt was inaugurated in 1933, the Volstead Act was amended so as to legalize 3.2 percent alcohol beer.

The dizzying pace continued as popular elections to select ratification convention delegates in the states produced majorities of 70 percent or higher in favor of repeal. Repeal of the 18th Amendment became official on December 5, 1933, after the Utah convention became the thirty-sixth state gathering to ratify the 21st Amendment. Prohibition—a powerful influence in the public life of Americans for nearly a century—disappeared thereafter as a national political issue.

Epilogue: After Prohibition

AFTER THE REPEAL of the 18th Amendment, liquor regulation did not end but once again became the primary responsibility of state and local governments. Although the new system of state alcohol regulation was more uniform in practice and more efficient in enforcement, it nevertheless resembled the basic forms of liquor control practiced at the turn of the century: prohibition, government control of liquor sales through state stores, or a system of licenses, taxes, and regulations to monitor retail dealers. Eight states continued to prohibit the sale of hard liquor in 1936, but by the end of the decade most of them allowed liquor sales. Prohibition remained in force in Kansas until 1948, in Oklahoma until 1957, and in Mississippi until 1966. More common was the adoption of government monopolies over the sale of distilled liquor, a system that has remained intact to this day in a few states. Most states, however, established a strict license system that limited the number of liquor retailers and controlled their location, hours of operation, and advertising. Most such states allowed local communities to bar liquor sales by means of local option. "Once it was carved back down to the bedrock of state and local option," the historian Morton Keller has aptly observed, "Prohibition . . . had more of a life after repeal than might have been expected."

Although legal drinking returned to most of the United States after repeal, the old-time brewery-owned saloon did not. By 1940 all but one of the states had enacted statutes barring the tied-house system. Beyond that, technology and cul-

tural changes had diminished the importance of the saloon as
a central drinking place for Americans. The development of
canned beer and the widespread availability of refrigeration
made home consumption of beer more popular. Men and
women together drank wine and cocktails at restaurants or
nightclubs. Bars, for the most part, were no longer exclusive
bastions of masculinity. Although some drinking places still
functioned as social clubs and cultural centers for specific
groups, the explicit ties between the drinking culture and the
political system died with the old-time saloon. As the political
and social significance that drinking had held in the nineteenth century faded, public drinking became but one of
a multitude of entertainment options for mid-twentieth-
century Americans.

The perception and treatment of drinking in the United
States after prohibition further distanced alcohol from politics. Scholars argue that the "disease concept of alcoholism"
dominated thinking about drinking after repeal. This view
did not hold the liquor industry responsible for the problems
associated with strong drink, arguing that most drinkers
could use alcohol responsibly. A minority of people, however,
were physiologically or psychologically unable to control their
drinking. These alcoholics needed to be the focus of concern and treatment, not legislation. Reaching back to the
tradition of the Washingtonians, drinkers in Alcoholics
Anonymous sought to help one another—by means of "experience speeches," discipline, and group support—to become
abstinent. Meanwhile, researchers examined the scientific,
medical, and health consequences of alcohol use. Discussion of
drinking moved to laboratories, scientific journals, and
church basements and away from Congress and state legislatures. The premier dry groups, the Anti-Saloon League and
the Woman's Christian Temperance Union, faded into obso-

lescence, quaint reminders of the powerful hold alcohol reform had once exerted over American public life.

Although Congress continued to tax liquor production
heavily after repeal, sentiment for a return to more rigorous
controls died quickly in national political circles. Unlike the
official hostility shown to brewers in World War I, in World
War II the brewing trade was considered a vital war industry,
critical to military and civilian morale. Brewery workers were
granted draft deferments, and 15 percent of the beer produced
during the war was reserved for the military. Alcohol had
been absorbed once more into the mainstream of American
life.

Nevertheless, even into the late twentieth century, the
image of prohibition remains a powerful, if often unstated, political presence. Depression and war have expanded the scope
of the federal government, to which prohibition stands as a
counterweight, a reminder of governmental limitations and
policy failures. To wary politicians, prohibition has become a
shorthand reference for the pitfalls of divisive moral legislation which should be avoided at all costs. On the other hand,
opponents of narcotics laws and strict government regulation
of tobacco, to use two recent examples, attack these government controls as "prohibition," using that loaded term to sum-
mon up memories of foolish, unenforceable, vindicative laws
that sparked massive popular resistance and a loss of faith in
government itself.

More recently, drinking has again emerged as a topic for
public policy debate and government action. After relative stability (between 2 and 2.1 gallons) since 1947, average consumption of pure alcohol in the drinking-age population
began to rise in the 1960s. In 1971 consumption reached 2.59
gallons, above the 1911–1915 pre-prohibition level, and surged
to 2.7 gallons between 1978 and 1982. By the 1990s the figure

rose to 2.8 gallons. Much of this increase seemed linked to the youthful culture of drinking that had overtaken the culture of male drinking in the twentieth century. On college campuses, underage and binge-drinking became serious problems.

Increased drinking and a rising highway death toll from alcohol-related accidents (17,126 deaths in 1996) revived grass-roots pressure for government action. Since 1980, Mothers Against Drunk Driving (MADD) has pushed for stronger penalties against drunk drivers, tighter sobriety standards on the roads, and cooperation from the liquor industry in encouraging "designated driver" programs. In the early 1980s the federal government withheld funds from some states to force them to raise their minimum drinking ages to twenty-one. On another front, a new emphasis on public health among alcohol researchers and activists has focused attention on moderate as well as problem drinkers. (Public health viewpoints have also encouraged the ongoing government investigations of the tobacco industry.) Critics of this public health sensibility label the new movement "neo-prohibitionism." Neither of these movements seek the prohibition of alcohol, nor are they mass movements on the scale of nineteenth-century temperance activism. But their concern for the safety and health of society—especially families and children—reflects, with a faint yet distinct echo, the insistent and recurring voice of American alcohol reform.

A Note on Sources

THERE ARE several excellent general histories of the broad sweep of American temperance reform. Jack S. Blocker, Jr., *American Temperance Movements: Cycles of Reform* (Boston, 1989) is the best recent survey by the acknowledged master of the field. Norman H. Clark, *Deliver Us from Evil: An Interpretation of American Prohibition* (New York, 1976) presents a thoughtful and challenging analysis that is distinguished by its sympathetic appraisal of prohibition. Joseph R. Gusfield, *Symbolic Crusade: Status Politics and the American Temperance Movement* (Urbana, Ill., 1963) is a landmark study by a sociologist that, although now dated in some of its assertions, alerted historians to the significance of temperance reform for American social and cultural history. For an informative survey of American drinking practices, see Mark E. Lender and James Kirby Martin, *Drinking in America* (2nd ed., New York, 1987). A valuable digest of local, state, and national liquor regulations is contained in Ernest H. Cherrington, *The Evolution of Prohibition in the United States of America* (Westerville, Ohio, 1920). Two good collections of essays are Jack S. Blocker, Jr., *Alcohol, Reform and Society: The Liquor Issue in Social Context* (Westport, Conn., 1979) and Susanna Barrows and Robin Room, eds., *Drinking: Behavior and Belief in Modern History* (Berkeley, 1991).

W. J. Rorabaugh, *The Alcoholic Republic: An American Tradition* (New York, 1979) is the benchmark work on the antebellum culture of drinking. Estimates on alcohol consumption in this book are taken from Rorabaugh and supplemented by *U.S. Alcohol Epidemiologic Data Reference Manual* (Rockville, Md., 1985). For a more recent analysis of the difficulties inherent in estimating alcohol consumption over time (and for a downward revision of consumption estimates), see Jack S. Blocker, Jr., "Consumption and Availability of Alcoholic Beverages in the United States, 1863–1920," *Contemporary Drug Problems* 21 (Winter 1994), 631–666. The importance of taverns in the social and political structure of early America is developed in David W. Conroy, *In Public Houses: Drink and the Revolution of Authority in Colonial Massachusetts* (Chapel Hill, 1995) and Daniel B. Thorp, "Tavern Culture on the Southern Colonial Frontier: Rowan County, North Carolina, 1753–1776," *Journal of Southern History* 62 (November 1996), 661–688. Peter Way, *Common Labour: Workers and the Digging of North American Canals, 1780–1860* (New York, 1993) vividly portrays the drinking practices of canal workers. For liquor and violence in the early nineteenth century, see Paul A. Gilje, *The Road to Mobocracy: Popular Disorder in New York City, 1763–1834* (Chapel Hill, 1987).

Ian Tyrrell, *Sobering Up: From Temperance to Prohibition in Antebellum America, 1800–1860* (Westport, Conn., 1979) is the best history of antebellum temperance reform. Still useful is John A. Krout, *The Origins of Prohibition* (New York, 1925). Two excellent local studies are Jed Dannenbaum, *Drink and Disorder: Temperance Reform in Cincinnati from the Washingtonian Revival to the WCTU* (Urbana, Ill., 1984) and Robert L. Hampel, *Temperance and Prohibition in Massachusetts, 1813–1852* (Ann Arbor, 1982). Placing temperance within the context of other reforms are Steven Mintz, *Moralists and Modernizers: America's Pre-Civil War Reformers* (Baltimore, 1995) and Ronald G. Walters, *American Reformers, 1815–1860* (2nd ed., New York, 1997). For the impact of the Second Great Awakening, see Robert Abzug, *Cosmos Crumbling: American Reform and the Religious Imagination* (New York, 1994) and Whitney R. Cross, *The Burned-Over District: The Social and Intellectual History of Enthusiastic Religion in Western New York, 1800–1850* (Ithaca, 1950). For a case study of the interconnections between the market revolution, revivals, and temperance, see Paul E. Johnson, *A Shopkeepers' Millennium: Society and Revivals in Rochester, New York, 1815–1837* (New York, 1978).

Robert J. Carwardine, *Evangelicals and Politics in Antebellum America* (New Haven, 1993), charts the political involvement of evangelical temperance folk. On temperance activism among antebellum women, see Lori D. Ginzberg, *Women and the Work of Benevolence: Morality, Politics, and Class in the 19th-Century United States* (New Haven, 1990) and Ruth M. Alexander, "'We Are Engaged as a Band of Sisters': Class and Domesticity in the Washingtonian Temperance Movement, 1840–1850," *Journal of American History* 75 (December 1988), 763–785.

For the political context of antebellum temperance and prohibition reform, see Harry L. Watson, *Liberty and Power: The Politics of Jacksonian America* (New York, 1990); Ronald P. Formisano, *The Transformation of Political Culture: Massachusetts Parties, 1790s–1840s* (New York, 1983); Daniel Walker Howe, *The Political Culture of the American Whigs* (Chicago, 1979); Formisano, *The Birth of Mass Political Parties, Michigan, 1827–1861* (Princeton, 1971); and William E. Gienapp, *The Origins of the Republican Party, 1852–1856* (New York, 1987). A compelling case for the importance of 1850s prohibition statutes in American legal discourse is made in William J. Novak, *The People's Welfare: Law and Regulation in Nineteenth-Century America* (Chapel Hill, 1996). The Know-Nothings are examined in Tyler Anbinder, *Nativism and Slavery: The Northern Know Nothings and the Politics of the 1850s* (New York, 1992). For the South, see Ian Tyrrell, "Drink and Temperance in the Antebellum South: An Overview and Interpretation," *Journal of Southern History* 48 (November 1982), 485–510. Frank L. Byrne, *Prophet of Prohibition: Neal Dow and His Crusade* (Madison, Wisc., 1961) analyzes the architect of the Maine Law.

Gilded Age politics and governance are covered in Morton Keller, *Affairs of State: Public Life in Late Nineteenth Century America* (Cambridge, Mass., 1977) and Paul Kleppner, *The Third Electoral System, 1853–1892: Parties, Voters, and Political Cultures* (Chapel Hill, 1979). For prohibition in Massachusetts after the Civil War, see Dale Baum, *The Civil War Party System: The Case of Massachusetts, 1848–1876* (Chapel Hill, 1984) and Roger Lane, *Policing the City: Boston, 1822–1885* (Cambridge, Mass., 1967). The most thorough examination of the Women's Crusade is Jack S. Blocker, Jr., *"Give to the Winds Thy Fears": The Women's Temperance Crusade, 1873–1874* (Westport, Conn., 1985); see also Dannenbaum, *Drink and Disorder*, and Barbara Leslie Epstein, *The Politics of Domesticity* (Middletown, Conn., 1981). For a crippling weakness in the Good Templars, see David M. Fahey, *Temperance and Racism: John Bull, Johnny Reb, and the Good Templars* (Lexington, Ky., 1996). David Brundage, "The Producing Classes and the Saloon: Denver in the 1880s," *Labor History* 26 (Winter 1985), 29–52, is a good account of radical working-class opposition to the social and political functions of urban saloons.

For saloons, see Perry R. Duis, *The Saloon: Public Drinking in Chicago and Boston, 1880–1920* (Urbana, Ill., 1983); Madelon Powers, *Faces Along the Bar: Lore and Order in the Workingman's Saloon, 1870–1920* (Chicago, 1998); Roy Rosenzweig, *Eight Hours for What We Will: Workers and Leisure in an Industrial City, 1870–1920* (New York, 1983); Jon M. Kingsdale, "The 'Poor Man's Club': Social Functions of the Working-Class Saloon," *American Quarterly* 25 (December 1973), 472–489; Elliott West, *The Saloon on the Rocky Mountain Mining Frontier* (Lincoln, Nebr., 1979); and Thomas J. Noel, *The City and the Saloon: Denver, 1858–1916* (Lincoln, Nebr., 1982). Valuable contemporary reports include "Social Aspects of the Saloon in Large Cities," in John Koren, *Economic Aspects of the Liquor Problem* (New York, 1899); Royal L. Melendy, "The Saloon in Chicago," *American Journal of Sociology* 6 (November 1900), 289–306, and (January 1901), 433–464; and John M. Barker, *The Saloon Problem and Social Reform* (Boston, 1905).

The WCTU is covered in Ruth Bordin, *Woman and Temperance: The Quest for Power and Liberty, 1873–1900* (Philadelphia, 1981). Bordin has also written the best biography of the WCTU's leader in *Frances Willard* (Chapel Hill, 1986), but for Willard's own perspective, see Carolyn De Swarte Gifford, ed., *Writing*

Out My Heart: Selections from the Journal of Frances E. Willard, 1855–96 (Urbana, Ill., 1995). The impact of temperance on women's political activism in the modern period is well treated in Paula Baker's excellent local study, *The Moral Frameworks of Public Life: Gender, Politics, and the State in Rural New York, 1870–1930* (New York, 1991) and in Glenda E. Gilmore, *Gender and Jim Crow: Women and the Politics of White Supremacy in North Carolina, 1896–1920* (Chapel Hill, 1996); see also Michael L. Goldberg, *An Army of Women: Gender and Politics in Gilded Age Kansas* (Baltimore, 1997). For Willard and the Prohibition party, see Jack S. Blocker, Jr., *Retreat from Reform: The Prohibition Movement in the United States, 1890–1913* (Westport, Conn., 1976). The prohibition groundswell of the 1880s is analyzed in Kleppner, *Third Electoral System*, and Richard J. Jensen, *The Winning of the Midwest: Social and Political Conflict, 1888–96* (Chicago, 1971). Immigrant objections to prohibition are contextualized in Jon Gjerde, *The Minds of the West: Ethnocultural Evolution in the Rural Middle West, 1830–1917* (Chapel Hill, 1997). For immigrant activism spurred by liquor regulation in Chicago, see Thomas R. Pegram, *Partisans and Progressives: Private Interest and Public Policy in Illinois, 1870–1922* (Urbana, Ill., 1992).

The organizational society at the turn of the century is described in Samuel P. Hays, *The Response to Industrialism, 1885–1914* (2nd ed., Chicago, 1995) and Robert H. Wiebe, *The Search for Order* (New York, 1967). Morton Keller, *Regulating a New Society: Public Policy and Social Change in America, 1900–1933* (Cambridge, Mass., 1994) sets the regulatory context for twentieth-century prohibition. The most thoroughgoing case for business support of prohibition is made by John J. Rumbarger, *Profits, Power, and Prohibition: Alcohol Reform and the Industrializing of America, 1800–1930* (Albany, N.Y., 1989). Connections between progressivism and prohibition are documented in James H. Timberlake, *Prohibition and the Progressive Movement, 1900–1920* (Cambridge, Mass., 1963); John C. Burnham, "New Perspectives on the Prohibition 'Experiment' of the

1920's," *Journal of Social History* 2 (Fall 1968), 51–68; and Paul Boyer, *Urban Masses and Moral Order in America, 1820–1920* (Cambridge, Mass., 1978). On brewers, see Hugh F. Fox, "The Prosperity of the Brewing Industry," *Annals of the American Academy of Political and Social Sciences* 34 (November 1909), 485–489; Stanley Baron, *Brewed in America: A History of Beer and Ale in the United States* (Boston, 1962); and Thomas C. Cochran, *The Pabst Brewing Company: The History of an American Business* (New York, 1948). Contemporary investigations of saloons and drinking include John Koren, *Economic Aspects of the Liquor Problem* (Boston, 1899); Vice Commission of Chicago, *The Social Evil in Chicago* (Chicago, 1911); and *Preliminary Report by the Chicago Commission on the Liquor Problem* (Chicago, 1916).

The best organizational study of the Anti-Saloon League is K. Austin Kerr, *Organized for Prohibition: A New History of the Anti-Saloon League* (New Haven, 1985). Kerr is particularly good on the League's decline after 1920. Peter Odegard, *Pressure Politics: The Story of the Anti-Saloon League* (New York, 1928) best conveys the propaganda and political style of the League in its heyday. For a portrait of one of the League's most vigorous officials, valuable for its revelations despite some misleading passages, see Justin Steuart, *Wayne Wheeler: Dry Boss* (New York, 1928; reprinted Westport, Conn., 1970). An equally interesting (and self-serving) inside account of the Anti-Saloon League from a critic of Wheeler is James Cannon, Jr. (edited by Richard L. Watson, Jr.), *Bishop Cannon's Own Story* (Durham, N.C., 1955). A harsh appraisal of Cannon is provided by Virginius Dabney in *Dry Messiah: The Life of Bishop Cannon* (New York, 1949). A valuable primary document is the League's Blue Book by William H. Anderson, *The Church in Action Against the Saloon* (Westerville, Ohio, 1906). An enlightening study of the legal maneuverings of the League, which also offers forceful new interpretations of national legislation, is Richard F. Hamm, *Shaping the 18th Amendment: Temperance Reform, Legal Culture, and the Polity, 1880–1920* (Chapel Hill, 1995). Local studies of the ASL include Thomas R. Pegram, "Temperance Politics and Regional Political Culture: The Anti-Saloon League in Maryland and the South, 1907–1915," *Journal of Southern History* 63 (February 1997), 57–90; Pegram, "The Dry Machine: The Formation of the Anti-Saloon League in Illinois," *Illinois Historical Journal* 83 (Autumn 1990), 173–186; and Robert E. Wagner, "The Anti-Saloon League in Nebraska Politics, 1898–1910," *Nebraska History* 52 (1971), 267–292.

For the South Carolina dispensary, see John Evans Eubanks, *Ben Tillman's Baby: The Dispensary System of South Carolina, 1892–1915* (Augusta, Ga., 1950). The workings of the federal liquor tax are explained in Hamm, *Shaping the Eighteenth Amendment*; Amy Mittelman, "The Politics of Alcohol Production: The Liquor Industry and the Federal Government, 1862–1900" (Ph.D. dissertation, Columbia University, 1986); and Wilbur R. Miller, *Revenuers and Moonshiners: Enforcing Federal Liquor Law in the Mountain South, 1865–1900* (Chapel Hill, 1991). The often haphazard regulation by the federal government of liquor sales to Indians is covered by William E. Unrau, *White Man's Wicked Water: The Alcohol Trade and Prohibition in Indian Country* (Lawrence, Kans., 1996) and Frederick E. Hoxie, *A Final Promise: The Campaign to Assimilate the Indians, 1880–1920* (New York, 1984).

The relationship of prohibition to Southern progressivism is ably analyzed in William A. Link, *The Paradox of Southern Progressivism* (Chapel Hill, 1992) and Dewey W. Grantham, *Southern Progressivism: The Reconciliation of Progress and Tradition* (Knoxville, 1983); see also Pegram, "Temperance Politics and Regional Political Culture." The potent impact of race on Southern progressivism is stressed in Jack Temple Kirby, *Darkness at the Dawning: Race and Reform in the Progressive South* (Philadelphia, 1972). Published state studies of prohibition include Daniel Jay Whitener, *Prohibition in North Carolina, 1715–1945* (Chapel Hill, 1945); James Benson Sellers, *The Prohibition Movement in Al-*

abama, 1702 to 1943 (Chapel Hill, 1943); Paul E. Isaac, *Prohibition and Politics: Turbulent Decades in Tennessee, 1885–1920* (Knoxville, 1965); C. C. Pearson and J. Edwin Hendricks, *Liquor and Anti-Liquor in Virginia, 1619–1919* (Durham, N.C., 1967); Henry C. Ferrell, Jr., "Prohibition, Reform, and Politics in Virginia, 1895–1916," in *Studies in the History of the South, 1875–1922* (Greenville, N.C., 1966); Jimmie Lewis Franklin, *Born Sober: Prohibition in Oklahoma, 1907–1959* (Norman, 1971); Lewis L. Gould, *Progressives and Prohibitionists: Texas Democrats in the Wilson Era* (Austin, Tex., 1973); Norman H. Clark, *The Dry Years: Prohibition and Social Change in Washington* (Seattle, 1965); Robert S. Bader, *Prohibition in Kansas* (Lawrence, Kans., 1986); Gilman M. Ostrander, *The Prohibition Movement in California, 1848–1933* (Berkeley, 1957); (for Michigan) Larry Engelmann, *Intemperance: The Lost War Against Liquor* (New York, 1979). There are also several excellent unpublished studies, the best of which are Earl C. Kaylor, Jr., "The Prohibition Movement in Pennsylvania, 1865–1920" (Ph.D. dissertation, Pennsylvania State University, 1963); Thomas H. Appleton, Jr., "'Like Banquo's Ghost': The Emergence of the Prohibition Issue in Kentucky Politics" (Ph.D. dissertation, University of Kentucky, 1981); and Robert A. Hohner, "Prohibition and Virginia Politics, 1901–1916" (Ph.D. dissertation, Duke University, 1965).

The best study of national prohibition is Andrew Sinclair, *Prohibition: The Era of Excess* (London, 1962). Sinclair's book is detailed and incisive, but it also reflects an older historiographical tradition that has been significantly altered by the scholarship of the last thirty-five years. Sean Dennis Cashman, *Prohibition: The Lie of the Land* (New York, 1981) is more recent but veers toward the anecdotal rather than the analytical. The newest popular account, Edward Behr, *Prohibition: Thirteen Years That Changed America* (New York, 1996), does not make use of the relevant scholarly literature. A modern interpretation of national prohibition that incorporates the insights of newer scholarship is needed.

Charles Merz, *The Dry Decade* (New York, 1930) is an excellent period piece, insightful and full of useful detail, but it was written as the prohibition story was still unfolding.

Topics related to the onset of national prohibition during World War I have fared better at the hands of historians. Christopher N. May, *In the Name of War: Judicial Review and the War Powers Since 1918* (Cambridge, Mass., 1989) is very good on the relationship between the war and prohibition. The National German-American Alliance is treated in Nuala M. Drescher, "The Opposition to Prohibition, 1900–1919" (Ph.D. dissertation, University of Delaware, 1964); Frederick C. Luebke, *Bonds of Loyalty: German-Americans and World War I* (DeKalb, Ill., 1974); and, in a local context, David W. Detjen, *The Germans in Missouri, 1900–1918: Prohibition, Neutrality, and Assimilation* (Columbia, Mo., 1985). A series of articles by Wayne Wheeler in the *New York Times*, March 28–April 4, 1926, are useful on legislative maneuvering by the Anti-Saloon League. Hamm, *Shaping the Eighteenth Amendment*, and Kerr, *Organized for Prohibition* are indispensable guides to the process. Despite his outdated tone (as evidenced in his discussion of the "feminine illogic" of women suffragists), Seward W. Livermore provides a good account of the wartime Congress in *Politics Is Adjourned: Woodrow Wilson and the War Congress, 1916–1918* (Middletown, Conn., 1966). Unfortunately, Arthur S. Link's monumental five-volume biography *Wilson* concludes with the declaration of war in April 1917 and so offers little detail on Wilson's attitude toward prohibition.

The best source on the enforcement of national prohibition by federal and state authorities is the five-volume study by the National Commission on Law Observance and Enforcement, *Enforcement of the Prohibition Laws* (Washington, D.C., 1931), better known as the Wickersham Commission Report. Strongly criticized at the time of its release for its ambivalent conclusions, the report is nevertheless an able analysis of the workings of prohibition and is unsurpassed for its wealth of detailed evidence on attitudes and behavior concerning the 18th Amendment. "Prohibition and Its Enforcement," *Annals of the American Academy of Political and Social Science* 109 (September 1923) and "Prohibition: A National Experiment," *Annals* 163 (September 1932) contain insightful articles. The best secondary studies of state-level enforcement are Engelmann, *Intemperance*, and Ostrander, *Prohibition Movement in California*. A lively account of the illegal liquor traffic is contained in Allan S. Everest, *Rum Across the Border: The Prohibition Era in Northern New York* (Syracuse, 1978). Malcolm F. Willoughby, *Rum War at Sea* (Washington, D.C., 1964) details the actions of the Coast Guard against liquor smugglers. The best contemporary defense of the prohibition record is Irving Fisher, *Prohibition at Its Worst* (New York, 1926).

The powerful impact of prohibition on the Democratic party is well treated in Douglas B. Craig, *After Wilson: The Struggle for the Democratic Party, 1920–1934* (Chapel Hill, 1992). Craig is also good on the AAPA and the American Liberty League. Another helpful work is David Burner, *The Politics of Provincialism: The Democratic Party in Transition, 1918–1932* (New York, 1967). Bishop Cannon's campaign against Al Smith is nicely summarized in two articles: Michael S. Patterson, "The Fall of a Bishop: James Cannon, Jr., *Versus* Carter Glass, 1909–1934," *Journal of Southern History* 39 (November 1973), 493–518, and James R. Sweeney, "Rum, Romanism, and Virginia Democrats: The Party Leaders and the Campaign of 1928," *Virginia Magazine of History and Biography* 90 (October 1982), 403–431. A good study of Herbert Hoover is David Burner, *Herbert Hoover: A Public Life* (New York, 1979).

Among the books that offer insight into the relationship between prohibition and the Ku Klux Klan are Leonard J. Moore, *Citizen Klansmen: The Ku Klux Klan in Indiana, 1921–1928* (Chapel Hill, 1991); Nancy MacLean, *Behind the Mask of Chivalry: The Making of the Second Ku Klux Klan* (New York, 1994); Kathleen M. Blee, *Women of the Klan: Racism and Gender in the 1920s* (Berkeley, 1991); Shawn Lay, *Hooded Knights on the Niagara: The Ku Klux Klan in Buffalo, New York* (New York,

1995); Kenneth T. Jackson, *The Ku Klux Klan in the City,*
1915–1930 (New York, 1967); and Charles C. Alexander, *The Ku*
Klux Klan in the Southwest (Lexington, Ky., 1965). Humbert S.
Nelli, *The Business of Crime: Italians and Syndicate Crime in the*
United States (New York, 1976) examines bootlegging gangs.

An excellent study of the Association Against the Prohibition
Amendment and the repeal of prohibition is David E. Kyvig, *Re-*
pealing National Prohibition (Chicago, 1979). Kyvig's book is also
the single best analysis of the decline of prohibition in general.
Kenneth D. Rose, *American Women and the Repeal of Prohibition*
(New York, 1996) provides more detail than Kyvig supplies on
the Women's Organization for National Prohibition Reform, but
not as much insight. For a solid short appraisal of the WONPR,
see Caryn E. Neumann, "The End of Gender Solidarity: The
History of the Women's Organization for National Prohibition
Reform in the United States, 1929–1933," *Journal of Women's His-*
tory 9 (Summer 1997), 31–51. Dry criticism of the repeal groups is
acidly presented in Fletcher Dobyns, *The Amazing Story of Re-*
peal: An Exposé of the Power of Propaganda (Chicago, 1940).
Dobyns popularized the view that a selfish desire to reduce their
tax obligations motivated the wealthy members of the AAPA.

A good case study of how gender-related attitudes toward
drinking shifted during prohibition is Mary Murphy, "Bootlegging Mothers and Drinking Daughters: Gender and Prohibition
in Butte, Montana," *American Quarterly* 46 (June 1994), 174–194.
Paula S. Fass, *The Damned and the Beautiful: American Youth in*
the 1920s (New York, 1977) is insightful on youthful drinking.
The role of prohibition in the public emergence of gay culture is
thoroughly explored in George Chauncey, *Gay New York: Gen-*
der, Urban Culture, and the Making of the Gay Male World,
1890–1940 (New York, 1994).

An insightful look at the legacy of prohibition is Joseph R.
Gusfield, "Prohibition: The Impact of Political Utopianism," in
John Braeman, Robert H. Bremner, and David Brody, eds.,
Change and Continuity in Twentieth-Century America (Columbus,

Ohio, 1968). American policy toward liquor in World War II is described by Jay L. Rubin, "The Wet War: American Liquor Control, 1941–1945," in Blocker, *Alcohol, Reform and Society*. An extremely provocative and controversial argument for the centrality of prohibition repeal in the rise and commercialization of the "minor vices" in popular culture is presented by John C. Burnham in *Bad Habits: Drinking, Smoking, Taking Drugs, Gambling, Sexual Misbehavior, and Swearing in American History* (New York, 1993). In a sophisticated and scholarly presentation, Burnham contends that the "minor vice" industry helped popularize working-class (Burnham calls them "lower-order parochial") patterns of behavior among middle-class Americans over the last six decades.

Index

A NOTE ON THE AUTHOR

Thomas R. Pegram is associate professor of history at Loyola College in Baltimore, Maryland. Born in Hammond, Indiana, he studied at Santa Clara University and Brandeis, where he received a Ph.D. in American history. He has also written *Partisans and Progressives: Private Interest and Public Policy in Illinois, 1870–1922.*